RAY ROBERTSON

WHY NOT?

Fifteen Reasons to Live

Essays

BIBLIOASIS

FIRST EDITION

Library and Archives Canada Cataloguing in Publication

Robertson, Ray, 1966-
    Why not? : fifteen reasons to live / Ray Robertson.

ISBN 978-1-926845-27-2

    1. Robertson, Ray, 1966- —Mental health. 2. Depressed
persons—Canada—Biography. 3. Authors, Canadian (English)—
20th century—Biography. I. Title.

PS8585.O3219Z478 2011   C813'.54   C2011-903425-5

 Canada Council
for the Arts   Conseil des Arts
du Canada

 Canadian
Heritage   Patrimoine
canadien

 ONTARIO ARTS COUNCIL
CONSEIL DES ARTS DE L'ONTARIO

Biblioasis acknowledges the ongoing financial support of the
Government of Canada through The Canada Council for the Arts,
Canadian Heritage, the Canada Book Fund; and the Government
of Ontario through the Ontario Arts Council.

PRINTED AND BOUND IN CANADA

WHY NOT?
FIFTEEN REASONS TO LIVE

Mens sana in corpore sano.

—Juvenal

CONTENTS

WHY NOT?
FIFTEEN REASONS TO LIVE

"So you're giving me advice, are you?" you say. "Have you already given yourself advice, then? Have you already put yourself straight? Is that how you come to have time for reforming other people?" No, I'm not so shameless as to set about treating people when I'm sick myself. I'm talking to you as if I were lying in the same hospital ward, about the illness we're both suffering from, and passing on some remedies. So listen to me as if I were speaking to myself."

—Seneca

INTRODUCTION

Everyone knows that happiness is the only currency that counts. No one on their deathbed can ask for more than to recall a lifetime long and prosperous in pleasure. Of course, the happiness derived from eating an ice cream cone isn't quite the same as that gained from listening to Mozart, and only someone incapable of appreciating both would argue otherwise. (Although, admittedly, a double scoop of *Kawartha Ice Cream*'s Chocolate Cherry Cheesecake misses the mark only slightly.)

I am the only child of working-class parents, the perfect ingredients for producing a happy human being. Never poor, I never wanted for a warm house in winter or plentiful food on my plate, and so did not grow up foolishly lusting after gilded illusions of wealth and comfort. Never rich, I was never hampered by what polite society refers to as "good taste" (the right vintage of wine, the correct cut of clothes, the desirable sort of friends), a very burdensome thing when one is a novelist and the most precious commodity of all is time – to read, to write, to sit around doing nothing while waiting for the right words to arrive – something much more easily achieved when, though one might prefer a bottle of twelve year-old Macallan Single Highland Malt, a pint of Old Crow Bourbon will do just fine. Being an only child was the icing on the cake in the formation of my character: what I missed out on in not learning how to play nicely with others, I more than made up for by having my parents' undivided attention and in discovering early on how to be contentedly alone.

And, for the most part, I am happy. Quite happy. Most of the time. Periodically, however, even though happily healthy, happily married, and happily able to practice my chosen scribbling profession, I've suffered from debilitating spells of Obsessive Compulsive Disorder (OCD). Sufferers of OCD are like alcoholics in that there is no such thing as being cured. One simply learns to live with the disease day-to-day. Sometimes its effects are slight (*Am I sure I set the alarm clock for a.m. and not p.m.? Did I remember to turn the stove off before we left the house?*), and sometimes they're incapacitating. Imagine being afraid of going for a walk because of the mental exhaustion that will inevitably result from having to count every crack in the sidewalk along the way, and one begins to get an idea of what full-blown OCD is like to live with. In addition to a higher-than-usual rate of self-medicating drug and alcohol abuse (particularly among those undiagnosed), OCD sufferers also commonly endure depression, such a mentally and physically wearying disease making everything *but* the disease – work, social interaction, solitude – virtually impossible. Being obsessed and/ or compulsive can be a full-time job.

Ever since I was diagnosed with OCD twenty years ago, a combination of medication, therapy, and greater awareness of what the disorder is has allowed me to live, if not entirely disease-free, then predominantly depression-free. In the early summer of 2008, however, almost immediately after completing the first draft of my novel *David*, both obsessions (repetitive thoughts) and compulsions (repetitive actions) I hadn't suffered from with any significant degree of intensity for several years began to manifest themselves. One of the advantages of living with any disease or disability for a lengthy period of time, though, is knowing the signs of incipient illness and what to do to preventively treat it. Besides, I wasn't all that surprised.

One of the central appeals, for me, of writing a novel is very similar to that of reading one: one enjoys a lengthy, concentrated period of immersion in another world. Occasionally someone will admit wonderment at how one can sustain the interest and dedication necessary to complete a two or three year writing project, and although it's always a challenge to deflect an unsolicited compliment, I usually admit that writing novels is the easy part – everyday life is what is difficult. No matter how high your blood pressure and what you know you need to do to lower it, there's your novel. Regardless of how much you don't want to do your taxes, there's your novel. Notwithstanding the government, your neighbours, or even your own admittedly less-than-perfect personality, there's your novel. A novel-in-progress is an anchor that keeps the world's sundry winds of inconvenience, irritation, and abasement from blowing you away.

But what goes up must come down. After the exaltation of – finally, unbelievably – completion comes the equally intense sensation of abandonment. Not by you of *it*, but it of *you*. All-of-a-sudden novel-less, it's not now a matter of a mere skin too few; rather, it feels as if the foundation has completely collapsed, a fool-proof compass has unexpectedly gone dead, a suit of previously impervious armour has turned into something resembling full-body Saran Wrap. One can't help but recall stories of formerly cosmically-secure 19th-century clergymen driven to suicidal despair by their confrontation with Darwin's theory of evolution, one-time contented members of a celestial family brusquely transformed into sorrowful metaphysical orphans.

The time-honoured method of coping with meaning-withdrawal (novel-writing variety) is systematic alcoholic over-indulgence, a practice at which, after birthing seven books and with an already-inbred inclination toward dissipation, I'm more than adequate. It's also advisable to undertake as many non-novel-related activities as possible, which in my case usually includes part-time teaching, occasional book reviewing, and record album collecting. The latter is a relatively recent enthusiasm, the result of two record-store-owner friends taking pity on me during an earlier post-novel melancholic state by giving me a quality used turntable. In the last six years I've accumulated over a thousand records – a habit that has not only brought me hours of black vinyl joy, but also helped see me through the haunted hiatus of two subsequent novels.

So, aided by all of the usual means of warding off familiar postpartum inertia, day after dull day followed the next, each bleeding into the same meaning-sapped blur. This is the other outcome of being finished with one's novel: life becomes very, very dull. No matter what troubles an awkward transition caused or how frustrating it was to find the right voice for your protagonist, at least each afternoon at your desk was charged with insight, intrigue, and ongoing interest. "Life, friends, is boring," John Berryman wrote, but being the writer, director, and producer of your very own prose movie (as well as filling all of the acting roles) has proved to be a wonderful way of counteracting this boredom. Not having a book to write – because the bucket does need to occasionally return to the well; the field must periodically lie fallow – one is left with the world straight up, no creative chaser.

And for whatever reason, this time neither excessive socializing nor pedagogic blathering nor assiduous book reviewing nor record store scouring did the trick. Additionally, my formerly in-abeyance OCD made an unwelcome reappearance. Like many psychological afflictions, it's uncertain whether OCD's source is entirely physical, behavioral, or some crafty combination of the two. In my case, periods of relative inactivity – as when a novel has just been concluded – remain ripe for renewed OCD infestation, the lifetime manic-depressive and eighteenth century British poet William Cowper's words ringing especially true: "Absence of occupation is not rest; a mind quite vacant is a mind distressed." Yet no matter how hard I boozed, read, taught, or reviewed, the more I suffered from anxiety sweats and heart palpitations and the inability to concentrate because my attention was involuntarily given over to the endless, pointless hours of obsessions and compulsions that dominated my waking hours (sleep – a sure sign of any form of depression – being an OCD-sufferer's primary, if too-brief sweet relief from uninterrupted, never-to-be-completed counting, touching, et cetera).

People don't become depressed from merely having OCD – or, for that matter, from anything else external – but from the psychologically- and physically-punishing *effects* of OCD. Unlike many people who suffer from depression, not only was there nothing fundamentally wrong with my life, I couldn't remember any other time when things had ever been better. Which only made my inability to sit still or think about things other than those I didn't want to think about over and over and over again all the more enraging. Which, not surprisingly, only exacerbated the problem: concentrated anger directed at what you don't want to think about or do is just gasoline to the already blazing fire that is five-alarm OCD.

As the weeks and then the months passed, I felt increasingly as if something or someone other than me controlled my mind and my body. I felt helpless. I felt helplessly terrified.

So I sought professional help, and increased the dosage of my medication, and practiced all of the coping techniques I'd developed over the years, and reminded myself that I'd been trapped in miserable repetitive loops like this one before and that always, sooner or later, the cycle of obsession and compulsion was slowly but successfully broken; and one night I found myself thinking that if I didn't wake up in the morning I wouldn't be happy to be dead, but the idea of not being alive was a relief. Why not? I couldn't help asking myself. Why not die?

As much startled as scared, I redoubled my efforts at contentment, reminding myself of all of the many things (my wife, my work, my friends, a good book, good music, staring at the stars) I had to live for. That I *knew* I had to live for. Unfortunately, how we feel is a much more powerful indicator of what represents reality to us than what we think, and the glint of every good thing in my life was always shadowed by the depression my OCD had come to cloud me under. Trying to be happy is like trying to be tall or like attempting to talk your way out of a tautology. Oddly, what helped most during this period of suicidal thoughts (never oppressive, yet always there, like a cold fall rain that threatens downpour but only dampens and chills intermittently) wasn't a neatly tabulated list of all of the pros versus cons that life had to offer, but the actual idea of suicide itself. Much later, a line I came across in Nietzsche perfectly encapsulated it: "The thought of suicide is a great consolation: with the help of it one has got through many a bad night." Admitted as an option, suicide lost much of its ferocity as a solution.

Addicts have to reach their own rock bottom before they can begin the climb to recovery. Regardless of its surprisingly consoling powers, even just the whiff of suicidal thoughts was my personal low. I'm embarrassed that it took thoughts of taking my own life to motivate me to independently investigate the roots and treatment of a disease I'd suffered from for two decades, but it wasn't the first time that human apathy and a naïve trust in authority have impeded knowledge and progress. Equipped with just the right amount of motivating fear and the information-spewing power of the World Wide Web, I played doctor for the first time since I was six years old. What I discovered was almost as revelatory.

What I discovered was that OCD casualties suffer from a lack of serotonin, a chemical manufactured in the brain. That the inability of serotonin to reach the brain's receptor sites, or a shortage in tryptophan, the chemical from which serotonin is made, can lead to depression, as well as obsessive-compulsive disorder, anxiety, panic attacks, and even excess anger. That Sucralose and Aspartame, the artificial sweeteners used in diet soft drinks, among other things – including Diet Pepsi, my long-time writing companion – hinder the body's ability to produce and utilize serotonin. That any form of caffeine not only tends to deplete serotonin, but is also an OCD aggravator, because of its stimulating effect on the nervous system.

I felt like a fool. I felt remarkably lucky. Within a week of simply but radically changing my diet, I felt better, my formerly crippling obsessions and compulsions immediately declining in intensity.

By the late fall, my body slowly detoxifying (my wife said that my skin actually smelled different), my OCD symptoms softening, crumbling, eventually falling away, I returned with renewed concentration and vigour to the business of rewriting *David*, and actually began to once again enjoy some of the things that months before I had determinedly told myself were reasons to live, but that I now knew really were.

And so life goes on. For most people. Except that writers aren't most people. It's not enough, for example, for a writer to have a good time – it's not a complete experience until he or she has not only captured it in words, but explored just what it was about it that made it so wonderful in the first place. Which partly explains why writers often make for invigorating, if occasionally exasperating company. Watching a beautiful sunset should probably be enough. Fretting over precisely what colour combination it is and what it is about it that brings such peace of mind might make for an interesting piece of writing, but isn't the best attitude to take while holding hands with one's partner while observing said sunset.

After I'd physically and mentally recuperated from my self-poisoning, I knew I'd been provided with an uncommon opportunity. *Not* to write a memoir of my illness and recovery – this has been done, and done, and done, and usually from a retrospectively falsely sagacious point of view – but instead to write a book that explores two of life's most central and enduring questions (which are really only two sides of the same coined question): What makes human beings happy? What makes life worth living?

Although chemically-incapacitated at the time, and hence incapable of taking much of my own advice, it was, ironically, when I was sickest and attempting to convince myself of all of the good things that life has to offer that I was most capable of understanding the appeal of a healthy body, a clear mind, and everything that those things allow you to enjoy (the pleasures of art; the joy of solitude; the transforming power of love; the sanctuary of friendship; et cetera), things I was temporarily incapable of experiencing. When Heraclitus wrote, "Disease makes health pleasant," he's talking about a sensation we've all had at one time or another. Yearning for those things we don't possess, we appreciate them more than if we had them.

Later, mind and body mended, I asked myself what it was I had yearned for, the things I couldn't have when I was ill that I used to so much enjoy, that used to engross, that used to sustain. All of the things that came to shine so brightly in the darkness precisely because they *were* in the darkness. Fifteen reasons why one should live. Undoubtedly there are more; undoubtedly some of those I've chosen to celebrate in the following fifteen essays won't resonate with every reader. Here, I can only echo Henry David Thoreau: "I should not talk so much about myself if there were anybody else whom I knew as well. Unfortunately, I am confined to this theme by the narrowness of my experience."

I'm also confined by what I've read. I consider myself a fairly well-read person (strong on philosophy, weak on history; good on nineteenth and twenty-century literature, but, excepting Shakespeare and the ancient Romans, anything further back than the English Romantics a bit of a bibliographic blur), but certain writers' names will recur here, a simple testament to their impact on my life. Studying philosophy at the University of Toronto as an undergraduate, one was not-so-subtly discouraged from taking seriously what was condescendingly referred to as "wisdom literature" (that is, non-analytical, non-language-based philosophy). Philosophy as conceived by the Greek Stoic Seneca – "Shall I tell you what philosophy holds out to humanity? Counsel . . . You are called in to help the unhappy" – was seen as, at best, endearingly quaint, and at its worst, as amateurishly pragmatic and intellectually naïve. Which was one of the reasons I eventually migrated from philosophy to literature: novels of the best kind seemed to be a sort of philosophy co-op program in prose, a place where ideas could be put into action and tested for their real-life applicability and worth.

The writers I've relied upon in my life for both intellectual and spiritual sustenance and whom I repeatedly call upon in the following chapters – whether poets, thinkers, artists, or Roman statesmen – are philosophers in the most elemental sense. Seneca:

Philosophy takes as her aim the state of happiness . . .
[S]he shows us what are real and what are only appar-

ent evils. She strips men's minds of empty thinking, bestows a greatness that is solid and administers a check to greatness where it is puffed up and all an empty show; she sees that we are left no doubt about the difference between what is great and what is bloated.

If treating Emily Dickinson or William Blake or Cicero or Jonathan Richman as unswerving truth seekers makes me a highbrow middlebrow, then so be it. A life spent exploring and espousing what makes life worth living seems to me a lifetime well spent. Besides, I've been called worse.

Albert Camus was only partially correct when he wrote, "There is but one truly serious philosophical problem, and that is suicide. Judging whether life is or is not worth living amounts to answering the fundamental question of philosophy." But physical suicide is only one way of destroying one's life. To bodily exist, but to spiritually die – a condition whose evidence we too often see in the forlorn faces of those we ride the subway with or work with or even live with and love – is not to live as human beings should and can. "Death is not the greatest of evils," Sophocles wrote. "It is worse to want to die, and not be able to." *Why Not? Fifteen Reasons to Live* is not a book about why one shouldn't die; if it succeeds, it attempts to address a much more important question: Why not live?

WORK

Work alone is noble.

  —Thomas Carlyle

It's the first principle of writing because it's the first principle of life: show, don't tell. Flannery O'Connor liked to say that the reader won't believe anything that the writer merely tells him – he needs to be shown it. No one had to tell me that what my parents did for a living was difficult, dirty, and degrading. I saw it at the end of the day in their exhausted faces, their dazed eyes, their limp limbs. I smelt it on their grimy, sweat-stained work clothes. I heard it in their tired voices.

Worse than what it did to their bodies, I saw what it did to their souls.

My mother, at home and finally free of work for a couple of precious days, gabbing on the telephone to someone she worked with, talking about – what else? – work.

My father, like my mother, wanting me to study hard and do well in school because he didn't want me to end up doing what he did for a living (hoping, instead, that I would one day be one of the suited and tied factory management types that he and all of his friends at the factory distrusted and disowned), but unable to understand why I needed some place quieter than the kitchen table to do my high-school homework and why I didn't want the extra hours I was offered by my boss at Sears. And why would he? Working full-time since the age of thirteen, where would he have learned that the soft-rock favourites playing on CFCO and the dinging of dinner pans and dishes weren't the ideal environment in which to crack calculus' mystifying code, or that a few less bucks in my pocket today might translate into a more rewarding tomorrow?

Even I, although only fourteen and working my first job, didn't have much difficulty imagining the rot a lifetime of repetitive, soul-sucking labour promised. The rich soil and hot, humid summers of Southwestern Ontario mean a large number of "corn detasselers" are needed every July and August to remove the pollen-producing tassels, buses of high-school students paid minimum wage to walk corn row after corn row plucking the yellow tassels off of each and every stalk. The mornings are chilly and dew-soaked wet and the garbage bag you wear, holes cut for your head and arms, does little to keep you dry, though the afternoon sun is baking burning. But for many, including myself, it's the first chance to bring home a paycheck, visions of – for me, anyway – record albums, new clothes my mother wouldn't buy for me, and fast-food cash making the endlessly boring days endurable.

Sometime during my second week of work I woke up and realized I'd been dreaming all night of detasseling, eight nocturnal hours of plucking, plucking, plucking. Our central air-conditioning made my bedroom cool and comfortable, but while I dressed for work I could see the hard morning sun already warming up to its soon to-be blistering daytime temperature. I had to be at the schoolyard in less than an hour where the bus picked us up and I was already exhausted.

Although Philip Larkin was a librarian and not a factory worker like my father or a food preparer at a nursing home like my mother or a summer-vacation field worker like me, he wittily, if woundingly, said what I could only ragingly feel about my parents' lives and my own apparent future:

> Why should I let the toad work
> Squat on my life?
> Can't I use my wit as a pitchfork
> And drive the brute off?
>
> Six days of the week it soils
> With its sickening poison—
> Just for paying a few bills!
> That's out of proportion.

And it wasn't as if the Robertsons alone had a monopoly on work-begotten unhappiness. History tells us that William Blake never visited Chatham, Ontario, but you wouldn't know reading his poem "London": "I wander thro' each enchanted street/ And mark in every face I meet,/ Marks of weakness, mark of woe." Worst of all, it wasn't just the worn visages of those actually mired in the drudgery of jobs they didn't want that were so despondent. Yes, there was the giddy gallop to Friday's finish line, the *yabba dabba doo* relief of another work week done and the prospect of two whole days of blissful freedom glistening on the horizon, but how soon – how all-too-soon – did the fresh promise of the liberating weekend sour with sombre Sunday night's inevitable arrival? And how much happiness was really being reaped by the weekend's brief reprieve, by summer's annual vacation, by Christmas morning's glittering bounty, by an afternoon's dedicated shopping? As far as I could see, not much. Whatever diversions you got up to on your days off and wherever you travelled on holiday and whatever you received for Christmas were never as good as imagined, and the day after you blew your entire allowance at the mall, the glimmer from yesterday's purchases was already beginning to fade. It sometimes seemed as if people were actually, if not quite glad, then relieved to go back to work, back to the very same jobs they were only just grumbling about.

"Man finds nothing so intolerable as to be in a state of complete rest," Pascal argues, "without passions, without occupation, without diversion, without effort. Then he feels his nullity, loneliness, inadequacy, dependence, helplessness, emptiness." Given the choice of being bored or being bothered, humans seem to prefer the latter. I always hated to feel it – and I certainly never admitted it – but by mid-August I was ready to go back to school. At the start of every summer vacation I swore I'd never be so bored again – that anything was better than geography class and math homework – but August's heat and humidity inevitably brought with it a renewed desire to regularly have somewhere to go and something to do. Even if that meant having to learn about The Continental Divide and having to practice integers.

Once I had started working year-round – graduating from corn detassler to busboy to part-time retail help at Sears – there was no denying that, even if one knew that what one was doing wasn't enjoyable or even particularly worth doing (aside from the paycheck it brought, of course), it nonetheless often felt satisfying once done. Longfellow, in his simple but moving poem "The Village Blacksmith," captures this feeling of elemental existential satiation well:

> Each morning sees some task begun,
>> Each evening sees it close;
> Something attempted, something done,
>> Has earned a night's long repose.

No day is sweeter than Friday. Not just because it's payday, but because it signifies that one's duty has been fulfilled and one feels as if one has earned the right to relax. "Work is often the father of pleasure," Voltaire observed.

And sometimes – not often, and certainly not conspicuously, but sometimes – there was something else. I heard it in the excited voices of my father and his friends when someone's car wasn't running properly, all of them standing around the offending engine and offering suggestions about what might be wrong, what should be done to fix it, why someone else's prognosis was wrong, no one as pleased when a solution was finally found as when the trouble was spotted. I saw it on TV when Colombo would wrap his pit-bull mind around a mystery and refuse to let go until the case was solved and the criminal forced to confess. I saw it when I watched *Hockey Night in Canada* and marveled at Guy Lafleur whipping down the ice intent on bulging the opposition's twine or Tiger Williams slugging a rival tough guy into submission. I knew it from knowing Mr. Allen, my public school physical-education teacher, who, unlike any other teacher I'd ever had (or, for that matter, any other grown-up I'd ever known), always appeared to have a smile on his face, and, whenever possible, practiced what he preached, making up for the odd number on a dodgeball team and even doing the calisthenics along with the rest of us that weren't much fun but we knew were necessary if we wanted to be better athletes. Plus, Mr. Allen got to wear a whistle around his neck and a track suit to work every day. Even Colombo didn't have it that good.

Happy people are happy with the work they do. Obviously, though, there's a certain amount of luck involved: my father, forced by his father to sell apples door-to-door at twelve instead of attending school, didn't have the options I had growing up, opportunities built on the sacrifices he and my mother made to ensure I could go to university without the added worry of student debt. Emotional satisfaction wasn't an employment consideration when he joined Ontario Steel shortly after my mother and he married, the position that paid the highest wages to someone without a high-school diploma his central job-hunting concern. Matisse might advise, "Derive happiness in oneself from a good day's work, from illuminating the fog that surrounds us," but, then, I doubt Matisse's wife had a baby on the way and that he was short first and last's month's rent on their very first apartment when he offered up this particular nugget of wisdom.

Even less than fully edifying, entirely fulfilling labour can still deliver a portion of agreeable work's promise. Flaubert was, yes, the modern novel's first great dedicated aesthete, a man who begged to "die like a dog rather than hurry by a single second a sentence that isn't ripe!" but his perpetual epistolary encouragement to his friends to work harder was more often therapeutic than aesthetic.

Work, work, write – write all you can while the muse bears you along. She is the best battle-steed, the best coach to carry you through life in noble style. The burden of existence does not weigh on our shoulders when we're composing.

Do not brood. Immerse yourself in long study: only the habits of persistent work can make one continually content; it produces an opium that numbs the soul. I have lived through periods of atrocious ennui, spinning in a void, bored to distraction. One preserves oneself by dint of steadiness and pride.

I continue my slow work like a good workman who rolls up his sleeves and sweats away at his anvil, indifferent to rain or wind, hail or thunder.

Baudelaire, too, envisioned work as a kind of conceptual condom to help shield him from the disease that is often everyday life (often including one's own inner life). From his prose poem "At One O'Clock in the Morning":

Dissatisfied with everything, dissatisfied with myself, I long to redeem myself and to restore my pride in the

silence and solitude of the night. Souls of those whom
I have loved, souls of those whom I have sung,
strengthen me, sustain me, keep me from the vanities
of the world and its contaminating fumes; and You,
Dear God! Grant me grace to produce a few beautiful
verses to prove to myself that I am not the lowest of
men, that I am not inferior to those whom I despise.

Not only are several of Baudelaire and Flaubert's
respective injunctions to work unabashedly utilitarian, both
writers also championed work as an act of defiance, when
lethargy and/or physical or material impediments make it
difficult. Here, Flaubert is enjoining his mistress, Louise
Colet, to eschew public renown in favour of finding her true
self-worth in serious writing, but he could just as easily have
been championing the athlete who plays in spite of his or
her pain, the teacher who still teaches although sick and
fatigued, the nurse who comforts and helps heal in spite of a
recently broken heart:

I'll tell you which are your days of pride. When you're
home at night in your oldest dressing-gown, with
Henriette [Colet's daughter] getting on your nerves,
the fire smoking and money worries and other troubles looming large, and you get ready for bed with
heavy heart and weary mind; when you walk
restlessly up and down your room, or sit staring at the
fire, telling yourselfy you have nothing to back you
up, that there isn't a soul you can count on, that you
have been abandoned by all; and then – somewhere
underneath your dejection as a woman you feel the
stirring of the muse, deep within you something

begins to sing, to sing something joyous and solemn, like a battle-hymn, a challenge flung up in the face of life, a surge of confidence in your own strength, the flaring-up of work to come. The days when *that* happens to you are your days of pride.

My first experience with Flaubert's days of pride, if one does not count those times battering the garage door attempting to improve my wrist shot or adding a half-inch to my biceps through devoted barbell curls, was when I was eighteen and terrified of not graduating from high school. After dropping physics and calculus – or, rather, after they dropped me – I had only one option left: a correspondence course in American History. The trouble was, I started it in early January, and had only five months to complete a ten month-long program, with the all-important grade I would receive going on my university application transcript. Every night after my other homework was done, I would read and write and read and write, writing so much, in fact, I developed a hard callous on my right index finger. I'd long since hung up my hockey skates and football cleats, but if I could have commiserated with a bunch of similarly beleaguered students, I surely would have bragged about my callous as much as I had previously about playing with a sprained shoulder or a cracked rib. Instead I'd just occasionally rub it and smile.

Although by the time I knew all about Manifest Destiny and the Boston Tea Party and had graduated from Grade Thirteen I was seven years away from writing the first sentence of the first draft of my first novel, I had nonetheless learned a valuable literary lesson: there is no such thing as "writer's block" (an entirely imaginary disease afflicting both nothing-to-say professionals and not-knowing-how-to-say-it amateurs). Clearly, if you have something to say, say it; if not, don't. Having nothing to write about doesn't mean that you're blocked – it means that you shouldn't be writing. Writers, like many other fortunate people who make their living sitting down, tend to forget that, as Mordecai Richler wrote, "[w]e weren't drafted, we volunteered," and as a result, everyone "could do with less self-pity, less dollar-a-word complaining about the lonely craft and how hell is a blank sheet of paper." One of the few elite Canadian writers who had a blue-collar background similar to my own, Richler expertly punctured the pomposity of the so-called "artistic temperament" when he recalled how "[my] father, a failed scrap dealer, worked a lot harder than I do without anything like the satisfactions. On bad days, it's good to remember that."

And if one is fortunate enough to find one's occupational calling, there *is* a satisfaction, one so profound that it can't be achieved in any other fashion – or none that I've ever known. "Blessed is he who has found his work," Thomas Carlyle wrote; "let him ask no other blessedness." When I'm working – deeply, single-mindedly working – the only word that approximates the experience is *absorbed*. You sit down at your desk, you tinker with yesterday's words, you take the screaming kettle off the stove and make the first of several cups of decaffeinated tea, you look out the window, you tinker some more, you read a poem by Emily Dickinson to remind you of your responsibility to language, you successfully subdue the desire to check your emails, you discover you forgot the cookies to go with the tea, you tinker some more, and this time the tinkering leads you to the next line – a new line – which is like a climber's spike driven into the mountain side, giving you a foothold to help get you to the next level – the next line – and then to the one after that and the one after that. When you finally look at the clock, it seems impossible: you've been working for an hour and a half, but it felt like twenty minutes, tops.

The concluding lines of Raymond Carver's poem "Work" capture the transformation that occurs when the alchemy of engrossing labour has been successfully performed: "The fullness before work./ The amazed understanding after." And not only is it experientially rewarding; the end-product, being sanctified by one's absorbed, loving attention, cannot help but be enriched. "Pleasure in the job puts perfection in the work," Aristotle observed. Carlyle went one step further, arguing that "A man cannot make a pair of shoes rightly unless he does it in a devout manner." Keith Richards used to take his guitar with him into the bathroom. You can hear it in the best of the music he wrote during the Rolling Stones' creative peak.

Not everyone can (or would even want to) be a poet or a novelist or a guitar player – the world needs farmers and waitresses and bank tellers and school teachers and plumbers just as much. In its celebration of a world where every man and woman has discovered fortifying dignity in their work, Walt Whitman's poem "I Hear America Singing" is overly optimistic certainly, naïve possibly, but inspiring nonetheless.

> I hear America singing, the varied carols I hear,
> Those of mechanics, each one singing his as it should be
>   blithe and strong,

The carpenter singing his as he measures his plank or
    beam,
The mason singing his as he makes ready for work, or
    leaves off work,
The boatman singing what belongs to him in his boat, the
    deckhand singing on the steamboat deck,
The shoemaker singing as he sits on his bench, the hatter
    singing as he stands,
The wood-cutter's song, the ploughboy's on his way in
    the morning, or at noon intermission or at sundown,
The delicious singing of the mother, or of the young wife
    at work, or of the girl sewing or washing,
Each singing what belongs to him or her and to none else.

If Whitman's words don't portray how people actually live, they stirringly – and necessarily – celebrate how they undoubtedly should.

LOVE

Love's a gift that's surely handmade.

—Guy Clark

We don't choose them, just like they don't choose us. And yet we look like them. We talk like them. Our blood is born from their blood, our hearts and brains and lungs grow from theirs. Sure we're sure that the books we read are smarter, the music we listen to better, the partners we've chosen to share our lives with a more comfortable emotional and intellectual fit. But somehow, eventually, we all become our parents. Naturally, everyone makes their own inimitable contribution to the project of selfhood – my own father irritatingly whistles 50's rock and roll songs while he putters around in the garage while I drive my wife slightly batty by humming honky-tonk tunes while I do the dishes – but Wordsworth didn't finish his thought when he wrote that the child is father to the man: every child is, above all else, also a daughter or a son. And not just anyone's daughter or son. This is good, this is not so good, this is the way it is.

Biff is Arthur Miller's *Death of a Salesman*'s black-sheep-in-residence, the one member of the Loman family who resists and, we're led to believe, conquers the disease of success-lust that has claimed his father and his brother. Willy is every dad who works too hard, worries too much, and goes to an early grave for the sake of his kids in the hope that their lives will be materially better than his (while, naturally, setting the sort of example that will almost certainly ensure that these same children grow up to work too hard, worry too much, and go to an early grave). As an indictment of the American Nightmare that Republican politicians and other cheerleaders of consumerism like to dress up as the American Dream, *Death of a Salesman* still burns true. Its only significant weakness, in fact, is Biff's epiphany near the end of Act Two, when he announces that

> suddenly I stopped in the middle of that building and I saw – the sky. I saw the things that I love in this world. The work and the food and time to sit and smoke . . . And I said to myself . . . Why am I trying to become what I don't want to be? What am I doing in an office, making a contemptuous, begging fool of myself!

Beware of late-night television offers of multi-purpose kitchen appliances that seem too good to be true and characters in literature claiming epiphanic breakthroughs. As much as his own DNA, Willy passed on his fantasy of soul-soothing wealth and renown to his children. Sudden insights are never a match for a lifetime of hard learning, and it's difficult to imagine Biff ever entirely waking up from Willy's deluded dream. Just as we must be thankful for the virtues our parents pass on to us – a sense of humour, a love of animals, an ability to get the job done no matter what – we must also accept the vices that they hand down as well. ("They fuck you up, your mum and dad," Philip Larkin wrote. "They may not mean to, but they do./ They fill you with the faults they had/ And add some extra, just for you.") Accepting this – reluctantly, but eventually – is part of what is called love.

More significant than either the inheritance of a strong immune system or the burden of premature balding, however, is the unconditional love we receive from the moment of our kicking and screaming arrival. On the one hand, it's so simple, so elemental – so instinctive – it borders on the emptily involuntary. After all, even after they found the butchered and bagged bodies at the bottom of Jeffrey Dahmer's freezer, his mother continued to love him, insisting that while, yes, he certainly had some anger-control issues he needed to sort through, at heart he was still a good kid – he just took up with the wrong crowd, his father drank too much, the other children picked on him because he wasn't good at sports, he . . . A parents' love is bereft of the freedom *not* to love. And isn't any action without the freedom not to act inherently less valuable for this very reason? To do good, doesn't one have to *choose* to do good?

Maybe. And maybe freedom is overrated. Maybe love – real, absolute, unqualified love – is so sacred, how one comes to give it or to get it isn't all that important. When I was less than a year old I had the flu and was quarantined in the isolation ward of Chatham General Hospital. The doctor and nurses warned my mother that, as much as she understandably wanted to visit and make sure I was all right, it was important that I not see her, as quarantined infants will eventually adapt to their temporarily motherless situation but will become virtually inconsolable if they spot their mothers, and this can adversely affect their recovery. The hospital staff assured my mother I would be fine and that I would be able to go home before too long and that obviously they would call her immediately if anything developed out of the ordinary (very unlikely). Three times a day for three consecutive days my mother walked from our apartment on Taylor Avenue to the hospital to peek from behind a wall to look at me behind glass. Usually, she said, I would just be standing up in my crib, content to hold on to the rail and rock back and forth, feverish but recuperating, but she simply could not stay away. (And she never let me see her – not once – either.) I'm 45 years old and my mother still scolds me long-distance if I don't get my flu shot and worries when we visit Chatham that I look too thin when I know very well I could afford to lose a little weight.

Our final paternal inheritance, of course, is death. Andrew Hudgins' poem "Haircut" does what all good poetry does: captures the flux of existence in a finely chiseled, concretized moment. Hudgins' narrator begins by recalling his impatient, scolding father giving him a home haircut when he was a boy. Half a century later, the roles are reversed:

> But now it's his turn and he sits,
> hands folded on his lap, unsteady,
> while I, with tiny scissors, snip
> the gray hair curling from his nostrils

and from both ears; and, Jesus, at sixty
the death hairs really get their growth,
don't they? The scissors pinch his skin
and he tries not to flinch. "Sit still!"
I snarl, and I'm so horrified
I say it one more time. "Sit still."

As Tolstoy's Ivan Ilych discovered, it's easier to grasp a syllogism that says that because all men must die and Socrates is a man, Socrates must die, than it is to master the entirely different sort of lived logic that infers one's own mortality. Death can never be understood as an abstraction. Your father's once strong, now trembling, liver-spotted hands; the balding head and the bushy nose and ears; your caring for him and your shrunken, shriveled mother much as they, once upon a time, cared for you – this is death's true epistemology. Your father's and mother's and everyone else's father's and mother's. And, ultimately – miraculously – your own.

Yet, as Emily Dickinson wrote, "The Soul selects her own Society." Meaning, we all get to choose our second family, the one we'll spend the majority of our lives with. And just as there are three stages to life, there are also three stages to non-familial love. Not that everyone is fortunate enough to fully experience all three – I have a friend, for instance, who believes he's only in love when it's new and fervent and frequently combative. "It takes patience to appreciate domestic bliss," Santayana wrote. "Volatile spirits prefer unhappiness." Still, the addictive quality that is the delicious pain of burgeoning love is undeniable, as conveyed in this anonymous 600 A.D. Japanese *tanka*:

At times I wonder
    if people in the ancient past
        like myself tonight
Found it difficult to sleep
    due to longing over love.

As intoxicating as it is, however (and aesthetically rewarding – without it, we'd have only a fraction of the lyrical poetry and popular music we enjoy), purely romantic love tends to grow less compelling as both our physiological fervor cools and we grow more possessive of the time and concentration it inevitably commands, our attention increasingly directed outward as we age. "The storms one so enjoys in youth are tiring in maturity," Flaubert observed. "It is like riding: there was a time when I loved to gallop: now I let my horse walk, and the reins lie loose." Elsewhere, writing to the same correspondent, he advised: "you should divide your existence into two parts: live like a bourgeois, and think like a demigod." It's difficult to write a novel about the tumult of love when you're simultaneously engaged in a tumultuous love affair.

Without in any way diminishing the transforming power of passionate flesh-on-flesh love – "The sexual embrace can only be compared with music and prayer," Marcus Aurelius observed – lust is pale ale compared to the full-bodied buzz of love. "Love comforteth like sunshine after rain,/" Shakespeare wrote. "But lust's effect is tempest after sun;/ Love's gentle spring doth always fresh remain,/ Lust's winter comes ere summer half be done;/ Love surfeit's not, Lust like a glutton dies,/ Love is all truth, Lust full of forged lies."

The real indicator of how high or low this or that lover rates in your life's scorebook isn't who was the better kisser, but the degree to which this or that person helped make you you. The you that *you* wanted to be. "i am through you so i," e.e. cummings wrote, brilliantly encapsulating the ideal symbiosis that exists between mutually supportive lovers, whereby one not only acknowledges and respects the other as a separate and unique person (which is hard enough sometimes), but actually actively assists them, as far as anyone can, in becoming the person *they* aspire to be. The foundation of this acceptance and encouragement of the other is akin to what Martin Buber meant when he distinguished between I-It and I-Thou relationships, and what Simone Weil meant when she wrote, "Belief in the existence of other human beings as such is love." It's tempting – and, given our basic, probably unchangeable egocentric nature, perhaps even unavoidable – to treat other human beings as a means to an end: specifically, our own ends. But to have someone thank you for helping them be happier in their life – however *they* define happiness – is the highest interpersonal compliment one can receive.

I wouldn't be a novelist if it wasn't for my wife ("Why don't you write?" she'd suggested when I was free of my philosophy degree and suitably existentially lost. "You're always reading and jotting things down in that notebook anyway." I would have never had the foresight or the audacity to begin otherwise). I wanted to live in the United States for awhile and get paid to go to graduate school while I hid from the nine-to-five working world and laboured on my first novel, and she came with me (but not before making me promise to make some of her own dreams come true while we were down south: to get a dog, have a garden, and rent a house large enough that, as usual, she'd have a painting studio of her own). I always wanted to wear sideburns, but never thought I could pull them off ("Don't be silly," she said. "And if you're going to have them, make them so you can really see them, don't wimp out"). I am through her so me.

And once you've lived in Wichita, Kansas, and San Marcos, Texas, and the novels get written and the paintings painted (and are still being written and painted) and variations in facial hair aren't quite the potentially life-changing alteration they were at twenty-four years old, one of the best things about being in love, you discover, is being alone together. Not having sex or making plans for the future or celebrating longtime goals finally achieved, but simply doing nothing together, the single hardest thing there is to do with another human being. Here's another anonymous 1,300 year old *tanka* and another pair of lovers oblivious to (or at least temporarily undaunted by) whatever wickedness and woe the world might conjure up:

> Since we are alone
>> Just you and I, my husband,
> What does it matter
>> If the moon does not appear
> due to high hills all around?

Because make no mistake: even if all of your professional dreams bear ripe, fleshy fruit and your personal life blooms just peachy plump and you own your own house and a summer place besides (and both mortgage-free as well) and passersby frequently comment on your dog's uncommon handsomeness, someone or something at least once a day will compel you to loudly echo Thomas McGuane's *Ninety-Two in the Shade*'s protagonist Thomas Skelton's exasperated cry, "Nincompoops assault me in squads." Times like these, to be able to (choose your preferred cliché) circle the wagons or man the barricades or lock the doors and bar the windows with your loved ones battened down beside you against the seemingly unceasing onrush of life's multitudinous mischief, is blessedly consoling. As Matthew Arnold commemorates in his poem "Dover Beach":

Ah, love, let us be true
To one another! for the world, which seems
To lie before us like a land of dreams,
So various, so beautiful, so new,
Hath really neither joy, nor love, nor light,
Nor certitude, nor peace, nor help for pain;
And we are here as on a darkling plain
Swept with confused alarms of struggle and flight,
Where ignorant armies clash by night.

Somewhere back in the fog of pre-gender-inclusive folklore it was said that a man needs a mistress when he's young, a companion when he's middle-aged, and a nurse when he's old. What a man or a woman really needs is someone who is all three and all at once, and all the way from the joyful, bubbling beginning to the sad, inevitable end. We probably demand too much of our partners – to be our chief confidante, our sole lover, our best friend, our ablest critic – and this is probably why sustaining a meaningful, lasting romantic relationship is often so difficult. But even an approximation is better than the lonely alternative.

And fortunate is the man or woman who can say, along with another long forgotten composer of another unforgettable Japanese tanka:

> If from your mouth
>   there hung a hundred-year old tongue
> and you would babble
>   I still would not cease to care
> but indeed my love would grow.

INTOXICATION

Stoned faces don't lie.

—Doug Sahm

L et us now praise alcohol and drugs. The sweet, soothing caress of alcohol; the mood and mind-adjusting
magic of drugs. After all, as Byron so sagely observed,
"Man, being reasonable, must get drunk;/ the best of life is
but intoxication."

But first a few words from the opposing point of view.

There's the argument that intoxication reduces human
beings to a state of physical and mental barbarism ("Drunkenness is nothing but a state of self-induced insanity," Seneca warned). There's the claim that intoxication is mere
escapism ("Drunkenness," Bertrand Russell wrote, "is temporary suicide: the happiness that it brings is merely nega-
tive, a momentary cessation of unhappiness"). There's the
contention that alcohol and drugs promise enlightenment
and eloquence while actually burdening us with babbling

incoherence ("One of the disadvantages of wine is that it makes a man mistake words for thoughts," Dr. Johnson sneered). There are countless tales of incapacitating addiction ("I had not taken a bath in a year nor changed my clothes or removed them except to stick a needle every hour in the fibrous grey wooden flesh of terminal addiction," William Burroughs has recounted. "I did absolutely nothing"). There's the belief that alcohol and drugs are a certain path to self-destruction ("Dope never helped anybody sing better, or play music better, or do anything better," Billie Holiday professed. "All dope can do for you is kill you – and kill you the long, slow, hard way").

To all of which one can only reply, yes, but . . .

But the atypical arseholing behaviour that sometimes accompanies the enjoyment of artificial stimulants doesn't originate in the bottle or the puff, but in the person doing the drinking or inhaling. "Wine," Dr. Johnson pointed out, "gives a man nothing . . . It only puts in motion what has been locked up in frost." Seen this way, the intoxicated state is a spiritual X-ray. "Champagne," Graham Greene wrote, "if you are seeking the truth, is better than a lie detector. It encourages a man to be expansive, even reckless, while lie detectors are only a challenge to tell lies successfully." In other words, it's *you* standing atop the barroom chair loudly declaiming how no one loves you and how everyone's a soulless robot but you – *not* the eleven pints of Guinness you drank. If anything, the beer was simply the megaphone you used to ensure that everyone heard you. (Besides, in the end, how harmful is the potential addition of a little blather and bluster when, along with them, comes the joyful subtraction of so many encumbering insecurities and inhibitions? How many love affairs, for example, or lasting friendships or life-changing decisions – not to mention unplanned for, but no less treasured, children – would not exist if not for, as Luis Bunuel said, "tobacco and alcohol, delicious fathers of abiding friendships and fertile reveries"?)

And what's so wrong with episodic escapism? What's so wrong with occasionally welcoming, even courting, a comforting illusion (particularly if the realities one daily deals with – as a social worker, say, or a secondary school teacher or a police officer or an environmental lawyer – threaten to spiritually crush and curtail one's ongoing good work)? "What's drinking?" Byron asked in *The Deformed Transformed*. "A mere pause from thinking!" The prescient pause that refreshes. And who said reality is so consistently magnificent anyway that one would even want to continuously stay straight to better experience it? Not Thomas Moore:

> Wreath the bowl
> With flowers of soul,
> The brightest Wit can find us;
> We'll take a flight
> Tow'rds heaven tonight,
> And leave dull earth behind us.

Nor Jean Cocteau, who, in his *Opium: Diary of an Addict*, wrote: "Everything one does in life, even love, occurs in an express train racing toward death. To smoke opium is to get out of the train while it is still moving. It is to concern oneself with something other than life or death." Despite his periodic detoxifications, Cocteau remained unwavering in his support of his favourite drug. "Do not expect me to be a traitor. Naturally opium remains unique, and the sense of well-being it supplies superior to that of health. To it I owe my perfect hours."

"I drink only to make my friends seem interesting," Don Marquis said. Friends, fellow party guests, family members, in-laws. And it's not just our social relations who need chemical-enhancing once in awhile. "The sway of alcohol over mankind," William James noted in *The Varieties of Religious Experience*, "is unquestionably due to its power to stimulate the mystical faculties of human nature, usually crushed to earth by the cold facts and dry criticisms of the sober hour." William Blake didn't need chemical assistance to glimpse a world in a grain of sand, but since most of us aren't William Blake, we have big red wines and little white pills to assist us.

Intoxicants proffer both the possibility of incoherence and the opportunity for compensating insight and elation. Too much beer may inspire soccer hooliganism and long disquisitions about familial history, but it also might provide, if you are lucky, an intimation of ultimate reality. "Malt does more than Milton can/ To justify God's ways to man," A.E. Housman wrote. What comes most readily to mind here are the various deeper joys of intoxication: a sense of oneness with the universe; an intuition of the connectedness of all things; the ineffable but no less palpable suspicion of the mystery and barely hidden beauty of existence.

In an article entitled "Do Drugs Have Religious Import?" published in *The Journal of Philosophy* in 1964, Huston Smith, a professor of philosophy at MIT at the time, presented two accounts of two different "religious" experiences. One occurred under the influence of drugs, one without their influence.

Suddenly I burst into a vast, new, indescribably wonderful universe. Although I am writing this over a year later, the thrill of the surprise and amazement, the awesomeness of the revelation, the engulfment in an overwhelming feeling-wave of gratitude and blessed wonderment, are as fresh, and the memory of the experience is as vivid, as if it had happened five minutes ago. And yet to concoct anything by way of description that would even hint at the magnitude, the sense of ultimate reality . . . this seems such an impossible task.

And:

All at once, without warning of any kind, I found myself wrapped in a flame-colored cloud. For an instant I thought of fire . . . the next, I knew that the fire was within myself. Directly afterward there came upon me a sense of exultation, of immense joyousness accompanied or immediately followed by an intellectual illumination impossible to describe. Among other things . . . I saw that the universe is not composed of dead matter, but is, on the contrary, a living Presence; I became conscious in myself of eternal life.

Huston only identifies which testimony was which in a footnote at the end of the essay (the drug-induced experience was the former), the point being that the psychedelic experience shares many of the same features as the purely "religious" one. And even if a chemically-assisted state of rapture isn't an intimation of ultimate meaning but only a mere mixing of chemicals from within (your brain) and without (your choice), isn't this one chimera worth chasing? Isn't the resultant feeling of cosmic consequence that which the first-century Greek poet, Claudius Ptolemaeus of Alexandria, meant when he wrote:

> That I am mortal I know and do confess
> My span of day:
> > But when I gaze upon
> The thousand fold circling gyre of the stars,
> No longer do I walk the earth
> > But rise
> The peer of God himself to take my fill
> At the ambrosial banquet of the Undying.

All of which can be acknowledged while still recognizing that drugs and alcohol can also stunt, pervert, and even kill. The sloppy slope from being the occasional beneficiary of a liberating, chemically-aided epiphany to a dull-eyed, slack-jawed dope fiend is sometimes surprisingly swift and always painful to witness. Many a brilliant performer has rapidly devolved from being a musician who dabbled in drugs to a drug addict who dabbled in music (Sly Stone and his artistic degeneration comes most forcefully to mind). And even if the risk of this happening is no higher than, for instance, the rate of injury or mortality associated with sky-diving or white-river rafting or energetic sexual promiscuity, the hazard remains no less real.

"Everyone can handle drugs until they can't" was a saying popular in the Grateful Dead's camp, as dedicated a group of psychic explorers as ever existed. Jerry Garcia's nickname was the self-explanatory Captain Trips, and by all accounts the music he wrote and played for many years only benefited from his outsized but astute drug use (no one practices their instrument for five consecutive concentrated hours without drugs; no one plays spirited four hour shows without drugs; no one stays in the recording studio for twenty-two continuous hours without drugs). I was playing the band's *American Beauty* album just before I turned on my computer to write today, and I'm glad Jerry Garcia was high when he and his band wrote and recorded it. As I'm sure he was too; not just because he clearly enjoyed taking drugs ("For me, drugs are just like the softest most comfortable thing you can do"), but because the wonderful, drug-abetted music he made then is still vitally alive fifteen years after his bloated, broken-down body died.

Make no mistake, though: after being introduced to heroin in the mid-1970s, both Garcia's music and his body (and his soul) began to disintegrate. Physically – except for periodic intervals of detoxification – he was a drug-induced wreck: dangerously overweight (having to periodically buy new shoes because his ankles and feet would swell up so much); diabetic (once slipping into a week-long, nearly fatal coma); prone to nodding off and burning himself while smoking (and torching many a hotel room); scabrous; frequently filthy; lethargic. All of which might have been at least partially justifiable if he had somehow still been writing memorable music, but, a handful of impressive songs aside, no one except the most blindly devoted Deadhead would claim that this was the case. In concert, his previously always interesting guitar playing was often languid and rote (and, like most junkies who isolate themselves from everything but their dope, he rarely listened to any of the other band members on stage anymore, robbing the Dead of much of their legendary improvisational interplay). Even when enough heroin was flowing in his bloodstream to satisfy his habit, he frequently seemed to longtime friends uncharacteristically morose, withdrawn, even surly.

None of which is actually surprising when an individual uses drugs or alcohol almost exclusively as an anesthetic or painkiller. Which, according to Garcia himself, was the chief attraction of heroin, the main reason he turned away from less corrosive, more stimulating drugs like marijuana. ("He called [heroin] his vacation," Justin Kreutzmann, son of Grateful Dead drummer Bill Kreutzmann, recounted. "His new way to take a vacation for awhile . . . Because in his mind, with all the pressure from all the overhead, he couldn't stop playing.") Which sounds not unlike a million successful businessmen who need three stiff scotches before they can even talk to their wives at dinner and who collect expensive cars or holiday homes or mistresses just to keep themselves duly distracted and from collapsing under the weight of far too much spiritually unrewarding work and the ceaselessly buzzing banalities that go along with it. Numbing yourself with heroin or stuff-lust or love affairs isn't all that different, in either methodology or effect. In the end, an old Scottish proverb applies equally well to them all: "The man takes a drink. The drink takes a drink. The drink takes the man."

That Garcia was aware he was working too hard and too much for too little spiritual return only makes his addiction and consequent deterioration and death all the sadder, since he clearly knew better ("We've been running on inertia for quite a long time," he said at one point in the early 80s. "I mean, insofar as we have a huge overhead, and we have a lot of people that we're responsible for, and who work for us and so forth, we're reluctant to do anything to disturb that. We don't want to take people's livelihoods away. But it's *us* out there, you know?"). Unlike the average American "success" story who makes himself miserable with meaningless overwork and who overcompensates with whatever is found to best numb the tedium and make tolerable the toll, Garcia had once upon a time read the right books (the Beats, with their anti-materialistic, pro-individualism message) and initially lived the right life (in typical hippie fashion, doing what he wanted to do – playing music, for example – simply because he felt like doing it, and not because it was a job he couldn't afford not to do). Garcia knew that "Everyone can handle drugs until they can't," but what he didn't know – or, rather, knew, but couldn't act upon – was that "Everyone can handle success until they can't." Drugs weren't the reason he died at fifty-three of a heart attack while detoxing once again from heroin. He died because he didn't know how to live well anymore.

And a life well led that includes intoxicants and all of the good things they can deliver means saying along with Winston Churchill, "I have taken more out of alcohol than alcohol has taken out of me." Falstaff, Shakespeare's best-adjusted boozer, is fat, lazy, and easily made unfaithful, but is also a shrewd survivor who knows what alcohol can and cannot beget and is determined to drain every drop of goodness that it (and life) possesses.

> A good sherris-sack hath a two-fold operation in it. It ascends me into the brain, dries me there all the foolish and dull and crudy vapours which environ it, makes it apprehensive, quick, forgetive, full of nimble,

fiery and delectable shapes, which, deliver'd o'er to the voice, the tongue, which is the birth, becomes excellent wit. The second property of your excellent sherris is the warming of the blood, which before (cold and settled) left the liver white and pale, which is the badge of pusillanimity and cowardice; but the sherris warms it, and makes it course from the inwards to the parts' extremes. It illumineth the face, which as a beacon gives warning to all the rest of this little kingdom, man, to arm, and then the vital commoners and inland petty spirits muster me all to their captain, the heart, who great and puff'd up with this retinue, doth any deed of courage; and this valour comes of sherries . . .

Above all, Falstaff's character is appealing because he is honest – about his cowardice, about his sycophancy, about his debauchery ("Aye, sir; to be honest, as this world goes," Shakespeare has Hamlet say, "is to be one man picked out of ten thousand"). But even those who succeed in fooling the world's fools by appearing intelligent when they're merely cunning, serious when they're simply solemn, beneficent when they're really only polite, cannot disguise what it is that truly makes them happy. "No man is a hypocrite in his pleasures," Dr. Johnson discerned.

Cyril Connolly, the British literary critic whose work in the last century I rank only second to Edmund Wilson's for its acuity and elegance, and who famously remarked that "The true function of a writer is to produce a masterpiece and no other task is of any consequence," also said, "Oh, the joy of lingering over port and brandy telling dirty stories with men in pink coats while it snows outside!"

Now that's a man I'd like to have a drink with. Or two.
Or three.

ART

Without music life would be a mistake.

　　　—Friedrich Nietzsche

To begin with, a few things that art isn't.

Art isn't entertainment – although it must always be entertaining.

Art isn't an obligation – although there's as much implicit responsibility on the viewer's or the listener's or the reader's part as there is on the side of the artist.

And most of all, art isn't culture – although without it, there isn't any such thing as civilization.

"Culture," wrote Simone Weil, "is an instrument wielded by professors to manufacture professors, who when their turn comes will manufacture professors." It's also a tool employed by politicians and arts bureaucrats to propagate the middling values (social equality, tolerance, moral conformity) which, though necessary to keep an egalitarian society running smoothly, are anathemical to genuine artistic achievement. "In all great art," Wittgenstein maintained, "there is a wild beast – tamed." The primary function of culture, on the other hand, is to domesticate and encourage docility, whether it be in the form of middle-brow arts prizes that most often reward artistic and moral banality (books or films that dare to remind us that preju-dice is wrong or that war is hell or that environmental disas-ter is to be avoided) or by way of a broad viewing or reading or listening public that applauds (and buys in large num-bers) artistic products that, not surprisingly, mirror their own cherished beliefs, customs, and even appearance. "The best is the enemy of the good," Voltaire wrote. And if some-one says that sounds elitist, they're right. Arrogance built on achievement should be encouraged, just as conceit based on inheritance should be discouraged.

Even if one could formulate a critically impervious theory of what makes a work of art good or bad (or worse – mediocre), this is hardly the place to do it. Suffice it to say that the surest sign of an authentic aesthetic response is somatic. "If you want a definition of poetry," Dylan Thomas wrote, "say: 'Poetry is what makes me laugh or cry or yawn, what makes my toenails twinkle, what makes me want to do this or that or nothing,' and let it go at that." Nabokov, too, used the manifestly physical as the surest barometer of whether a work of art succeeds or not, noting how "the wise reader reads . . . not with his heart, not so much with his brain, but with his spine. It is there that occurs the telltale tingle."

My own first tingling encounter with the transforming power of art was by way of an eight-track tape of rock and roll oldies my parents purchased from Woolco. The country-pop I'd heard up until then on the local radio station that played incessantly in my mother's kitchen and what passed for rock and roll on network television (*Happy Days*, *The Sonny and Cher Show*, *Tony Orlando and Dawn*) in no way prepared me for the aural assault of Little Richard and Jerry Lee Lewis. Exciting or energetic or even aggressive doesn't come close to describing how the respective sounds concocted by these two performers exploded the ears and mind of an nine-year-old growing up in the torpid Southwestern Ontario suburbs of 1975. This music was different from other music. This music was rude. Defiant. *Dangerous*.

I'd close the spare bedroom door where the Sears Candle stereo sat and turn the volume up as loud as I could before the speakers began to crackle and snap and play my favourites: Dion and the Belmonts' "Run Around Sue," Freddy Cannon's "Tallahassee Lassie," Buddy Holly's "Oh Boy." My favourite favourites, though, were Little Richard's "Tutti Fruiti" and Jerry Lee's "Great Balls of Fire." These I couldn't simply sit and toe-tapping listen to: to these I was compelled to move, to shake, to use my hands and feet. My first air instrument wasn't a guitar, but an air piano, which I'd pound away at where the bed happened to be. It was fortunate that my keyboard was composed of only air and an eight-inch thick mattress, otherwise my fingers would have been too sore to hold on to a hockey stick.

Real rock and roll, I'd go on to learn, is unadulterated Id music – feral, lustful, shameless. Real rock and roll makes you do things tonight you won't believe tomorrow morning you did. If it's not slightly frightening, in other words, it's not the real thing. And in spite of over fifty years of artistically degenerative dilution, wanton trivializing commercialization, and simple overexposure, the best of Little Richard and Jerry Lee Lewis' music remains dangerous. The enduring anarchic energy of the Georgia Peach and the Killer's finest music (I remain incapable of standing still whenever I hear "Lucille" and am still slightly spooked by Jerry Lee's chortle at the end of "Don't Put No Headstone On My Grave") is testament to the wonderfully unfathomable mystery of art: how a slab of old black vinyl spun at 33 1/3 rotations per minute can somehow make your soul sparkle and give your arms goosebumps.

Powerful music (and powerful poetry, art, film, et cetera) transforms us into fools, holy fools; immersed in it, we tend to look foolish, to act foolish, and to allow ourselves to momentarily imagine all sorts of plainly foolish things, things like uncompromised happiness, aesthetic perfection, and spiritual purity. Jimi Hendrix's face when he played the guitar; Keith Moon's when he pounded the drums; Janis Joplin's when she screamed and begged and shouted; you when you miss your subway stop with your nose stuck inside a novel: each offers a passionate, pained portrait of a human being in direct, ecstatic communion with what Goethe, speaking of Mozart's music, called "the human incarnation of the divine force of creation." If you don't believe me, watch an episode of the *The Night Stalker* starring Darren McGavin, a weekly television series that ran on ABC from 1974 to 1975. I did. And it changed my life.

McGavin played Carl Kolchak, an investigative reporter for Chicago-based Independent News Service, who every Thursday night at 9 p.m. stumbled upon a different supernatural mystery in the course of covering a seemingly commonplace story. Although Kolchak would always singlehandedly defeat that week's vampire or killer robot or voodoo menace, his evidence in the case was always destroyed or seized, usually by a government official or major social figure who sought to cover up the incident, and his editor, Tony Vincenzo, would always refuse to print the story. The truth, as Kolchak unfailingly pointed out at episode's end, would once again be kept from the public.

Before I wanted to be a professional hockey player or a member of the R.C.M.P., I wanted to be Carl Kolchak. Kolchak wasn't just the one to drive the stake through the vampire's heart – he was usually the only person who believed that a member of the undead was alive and killing in present-day Chicago, something he knew to be true because – unlike the rest of the gullible press, the obedient, unquestioning police, and the apathetic citizenry – Kolchak had an open and intuitive mind and an ornery indifference toward anything but his story. Take the way he dressed, for instance – it never deviated from show to show. Every episode saw him in the same grimy blue pin-striped seersucker suit, blue button-down collar shirt and loosened black tie, a pair of old beat-up white running shoes and white socks, with the whole thing topped off by his signature straw hat with a red and black band (his only fashion accessories being his hand-held tape recorder and ever-present camera). More important than how he looked (a mess) or the car he drove (a wreck) or what he ate (usually black coffee and hot dogs) or what other people thought of him (Kolchak: "Exactly what don't you like about this hat?" Vincenzo: "What's under it.") was the story – the undeniably real, seemingly unreal story – and the need for it to be told, whether the world wanted to hear it or not.

I've yet to kill any vampires (although I have endured my fair share of zombies) and I stopped wearing white running shoes with white socks and blue dress pants soon after

The Night Stalker went off the air, but if I had never met Carl Kolchak I'm sure that I would never have become a novelist. Sure, the plots were predictable, all of the characters two-dimensional, and the monsters weren't even scary (and some, even to a pre-pubescent, were hilariously unscary), but that only makes it even more of a triumph: I learned to value the single-minded pursuit of the truth from a TV show about a ghoul-hunting newspaperman that was cancelled after a single season. That is, to me, far more mysterious than any extraterrestrial.

Of course, writing about the existence-altering power of artistic bliss is like talking about sex: discoursing is rarely as much fun as actually doing. Each is also extremely challenging to do well, the tendency in both cases being toward either the boringly analytical (ponderous, line-by-line poetic précis, for example, or equally tiresome sexual score-keeping) or else the embarrassingly rapturous (typical over-the-top boosterism or cosmic cum shots à la D.H. Lawrence or Henry Miller conveyed with about just as much subtlety). Much like the dilemma of the mystic who desires to communicate the essentially ineffable, the writer hoping to convincingly recreate and explore the – at their best – quasi-mystical experiences of the creative and the sexual needs to stretch and sever and reconfigure language in sometimes startling fresh ways, a virtual recipe for meager book sales and raised critical eyebrows. Dangerous – there's that word again – deeds demand dangerous words.

And the best thing anyone can say about any work of art, whether it's a novel, a painting, or a three minute rock song, is that it's dangerous. Not dangerous in the way that blaring The Doors' "The End" from your bedroom stereo might scare your mom, but dangerous in the way that Kafka defined all good art: as the careful application of an ice pick to the frozen sea within us. Genuine art speaks to no one else but you. Jack Kerouac spoke to me. Not necessarily in terms of what he said, but how he said it. His style spoke to me.

Defining literary style is almost as difficult as defining soul, but Llewelyn Powys probably did the job as well as anyone. "Style," he claimed, "is the ultimate expression of the author's unique spiritual consciousness. This spiritual consciousness has been arrived at through various influences. Ancestry has bequeathed to it a certain fundamental disposition, environment has thickened this congenital inclination, and chance temperament of each individual has flashed it into life out of nowhere." Georges Louis Leclerc de Buffon put it more succinctly: "The style is the man." To understand Jack Kerouac's style, I needed to understand Jack Kerouac the man.

Some have made much of Kerouac's Catholicism as a key to understanding his mature prose style, the act of confession understood as an oral embodiment of his theory of spontaneous prose, but Kerouac was more of a Catholic (that is, hadn't yet embraced Buddhism) when he wrote his Hemingway- and Saroyan-derivative juvenilia (and, later, his heavily Thomas Wolfe-influenced first novel, *The Town and the City*) than he was when his mature, "confessional" style blossomed. The first major building block in the development of Kerouac's prose style wasn't a religion or a philosophy or even a book, but the letters he received from a former Denver juvenile delinquent and future San Quentin inmate.

"I got the idea for the spontaneous style of *On the Road* from seeing how good old Neal Cassady wrote his letters to me," Kerouac said, "all first person, fast, mad, confessional, completely serious, all detailed ... Cassady also began his early youthful writing with attempts at slow, painstaking, and-all-that-crap craft business, but got sick of it like I did, seeing it wasn't getting out his guts and heart the way it *felt* like coming out. But I got the flash from his style."

Kerouac's finest work often oscillates between the appeal and limitations of the freest of free jazz – intoxicating freedom alternating with bewildering frenzy – and he is, above all else, a linguistic liberator, allowing – and, at his best, *compelling* – his readers to get off their asses at the back of the club and to pick up their own instruments and join him on stage, to play their own minds, bodies, souls, lives. Genuine art is never just about the artist. The penultimate paragraph from *Tristessa* – "I'll go light candles to the Madonna, I'll paint the Madonna, and eat ice cream, benny and bread – 'Dope and saltpork,' as Bhikku Booboo said – I'll go to the South of Sicily in the winter, and paint memories of Arles – I'll buy a piano and Mozart me that – I'll write long sad tales about the people in the legend of my life – This part is my part of the movie, let's hear yours" – is, in essence, an injunction to remember the songs that one has heard over the preceding 124 pages so that one may forget them and write one's own. Keroauc's best readers do. And have a hell a lot of fun doing it, too.

Naturally, readers – Canadian readers perhaps more than many others – can be excused if that particular three letter F-word isn't the first to lift off the tip of the tongue when describing exceptional literature. Not when award-winning books are routinely chosen for their socially benefi-cent values – as if art was some sort of high-fibre cultural bran – and an author being numbingly boring is more often than not mistaken for an author who's simply sturdily serious. No matter the amount of nudity in the films we watch or the volume of the music we listen to, we seem to like our art as we do our politics: bland, imitative, inoffensive.

I read Thomas McGuane's second novel, *The Bushwhacked Piano*, when I was twenty-five years old and not knowing what to do with my life. By the time I finished it, I did. I wanted to do what McGuane did: sing like a poet, poke and jokey-jab like an expert satirist, and ask all of the really big questions that most of my university philosophy courses ignored in favour of language analysis and symbolic knowledge. I wanted to have fun, in other words. *The Bushwhacked Piano* is a textbook of fun.

The story itself is slight, as are most of McGuane's plots, and similar in its essentials to the bulk of those novels that came after. Nicholas Payne flees his country-clubbing parents and their shimmering suburban nightmare in search of the open road, forbidden love, and existence-altering satori, just as long as it can be fitted in between an imminent hemorrhoid operation and the selling of locally-made bat towers to gullible Mid-Western Yahoos with persistent mosquito problems. Like any piece of superior art, however, it's not the tale that tantalizes, it's how the tale is told. Here's McGuane the master craftsman describing Nicholas' nemesis, Wayne Codd, spying on Payne and his girlfriend Ann making love, and in the process making a single sentence fetch, roll over, and shake both paws when most authors would need an entire novel just to get the dog to sit.

Hanging, later, upended over the dormer window of Ann's room, he watched her mock burlesque before Payne, their subsequent entanglement, her compact uplift of blushing buttock, his paler flesh and hers flaring in their seizure, the long terrific prelude and final, spasmic, conjunctive entry, marked, unknown to either of them, by the gloomy jetting of Codd against the shingles overhead.

But being a linguistic lion and a pretension-puncturing ironist doesn't mean an artist can't also be a significant thinker, all of which the McGuane of *The Bushwhacked Piano* undeniably is, a funky philosopher who knows how to lay it on the line as he lays down a line.

Payne poised a jackknife spread with peanut butter over a rigid piece of bread and lifted his face to the sea. He felt as if he had been made an example of; and that, even now, he was part of a demonstration, an exhibit. He held the knife and peanut butter steady. The sky rose over him, round and vitreous, a glass enclosure. He smiled, at one with things. He knew the great blenders hummed in state centers and benign institutions; while he, far away, put it all together at a time when life was cheap.

But then the abrasions, all the incredible abrasions, had *rendered* him. The pale, final shape of Payne, like the yolk of an egg held to the light, had come to be seen.

I am at large.

Because of Thomas McGuane's *The Bushwhacked Piano*, so am I. "The power of the visible/ is the invisible," wrote Marianne Moore. Sounds, stories, pictures: we are the art we love.

THE MATERIAL
WORLD

One real world is enough.

—Santayana

A friend of mine, the poet David O'Meara, is fond of saying, "I have issues with nature." My own ambivalence toward the material world is perhaps even more fundamental: even inanimate objects possess the power to unnerve me. John Berryman, someone else who spent the majority of his adult hours sitting on his ass while living chiefly in his head, once recollected to a television interviewer how writers frequently differ from non–writers in their relationship to the insensible world: "Some people certainly feel that it's the price you pay for an overdeveloped sensibility. Namely, you know, the door sticks, as I try to open it, it sticks. Okay, so I have a nervous breakdown. The guy at the corner of Fifth and Hennepin, the door sticks, shit, he fixes it and opens it. No sweat." I have fought countless battles over the years with obstinate and ultimately victoriously blinking VCRs, loose bicycle chains, uncooperative printers, unwieldy garden shears, missing single socks, immovable kitchen counter stains, and I don't expect my war with the material world to end until I do, with the final victory most assuredly not my own.

Then there's a world of hassles and heartbreak a little closer to home – you. Fleshy, fingertip-feeling, blood-and-bones you. When you're young, it's your acne, your gangly limbs, your too-thin calves; when you're middle-aged, it's your growing waistline, your receding hairline, your increasing cholesterol count; when you're old, it's your weakening vision, your fading hearing, your wilting energy. For Edna St. Vincent Millay, the human frame was often little more than a collection of irksome inconveniences:

> For the body at best
> > Is a bundle of aches,
> Longing for rest;
> > It cries when it wakes.

Delmore Schwartz went even further, dubbing his body the "Heavy Bear," and his poem of the same name ("The Heavy Bear Who Goes with Me") decries the body's ignoble demands and pathetic weaknesses, longing for a purer form of existence somehow independent of human life's corporeal constraints:

> The heavy bear who goes with me,
> A manifold honey to smear his face,
> Clumsy and lumbering here and there,

The central ton of every place,
The hungry beating brutish one
In love with candy, anger, and sleep,
Crazy factotum, dishevelling all,
Climbs the building, kicks the football,
Boxes his brother in the hate-ridden city.

Breathing at my side, that heavy animal,
That heavy bear who sleeps with me,
Howls in his sleep for a world of sugar,
A sweetness intimate as the water's clasp,
Howls in his sleep because the tight-rope
Trembles and shows the darkness beneath.
—The strutting show-off is terrified,
Dressed in his dress-suit, bulging his pants,
Trembles to think that his quivering meat
Must finally wince to nothing at all.

Torn dress pants and flat tires and an arthritic knee
that isn't going to get better: no wonder people believe,
against overwhelming evidence, in heaven or Platonic
Forms or The Future or whatever else promises eventual
happiness. How pleasant to believe that somehow, somewhere, at some point, everything is going to work out just
fine. "Imagination," Pascal said, "disposes of everything; it
creates beauty, justice, and happiness, which is everything
in this world." "The brain," Emily Dickinson wrote, "is
wider than the sky," and we can mentally fashion a celestial retirement home where everything evens out in the
end and everyone gets their wings and is reunited with
their long-gone relatives and cherished childhood pets.
Unfortunately, as Alfred North Whitehead reminds us,

"We think in generalities, but we live in detail." Every Saturday night is succeeded by a morning after.

Some, however, have avoided the danger of the idealist's hangover by being perfectly content with the secular pleasures of sober Tuesday afternoon. Walt Whitman, for one, didn't suffer the vertigo that often accompanies grasping after heaven's divine delights because he was perfectly content to exist in his very own heaven right down here on dirty old earth. And that heaven began with delightfully dirty old him.

"If anything is sacred the human body is sacred," he avowed. Foremost, one's own body: "and nothing, not God, is greater to one than one's self is." "I celebrate myself," Whitman famously declared – himself and all of the miraculous minutiae of ostensibly mundane everyday life. But Whitman wasn't celebrating simple egoism – Whitman's body and life are holy because your body and life are holy because the air you both breathe is holy and because all of earthly existence is holy, even that which "is commonest and cheapest and nearest and easiest."

> I believe a leaf of grass is no less than the journeywork of
>   the stars,
> And the pismire is equally perfect, and a grain of sand,
>   and the egg of the wren,
> And the tree-toad is a chef-d'oeuvre for the highest,
> And the running blackberry would adorn the parlors of
>   heaven,
> And the narrowest hinge in my hand puts to scorn all
>   machinery,
> And the cow crunching with depressed head surpasses
>   any statue,

And a mouse is miracle enough to stagger sextillions of
> infidels,
And I could come every afternoon of my life to look at the
> farmer's girl
>> Boiling her iron tea-kettle and baking shortcake.

Whitman's celebration of the contentedly finite individual, particularly as an antidote to arid and exasperating Ide-
alism ("Won't they try to square the circle," Montaigne
complained, "while perched on their wives!") is refreshing.
Like any fundamentalist, however, his corporeal cosmology
is one-sided, exchanging a reverence for the airy for an
obsession with the exclusively earthy. Montaigne shares
Whitman's distrust of the abstract – "They want to get out of
themselves and escape from the man. That is madness:
instead of changing into angels, they change into beasts;
instead of raising themselves, they lower themselves" – but,
as a beacon of sensible moderation, Montaigne acknowledges the human need for the Ideal as well. One of the keys
to human happiness for Montaigne is being able to move
back and forth between these two very different realms:

> When I dance, I dance; when I sleep, I sleep; yes, and
> when I walk alone in a beautiful orchard, if my
> thoughts have been dwelling on extraneous incidents
> for some part of the time, for some other part I bring
> them back to the walk, to the orchard, to the sweetness
> of this solitude, and to me.

Once the decision has been made to celebrate rather
than cogitate, simple good health itself has to rank foremost
when enumerating the pleasures of the material world.

Since everyone from time to time has been laid up with a bad cold or a sore tooth or a sprained ankle, all can agree with Virgil that "The greatest wealth is health." If the disorder has involved a close call with a potentially mortal disease or a near-fatal accident, the fortune one feels is amplified, the grateful survivor capable of truly appreciating the seemingly commonplace daily miracles that Whitman sang so fervently of, "the feeling of health . . . the full-noon trill . . . the song of me rising from bed and meeting the sun." As long as one's physical well-being doesn't become an end-in-itself – "People who are always taking care of their health are like misers who are hoarding a treasure which they have never spirit enough to enjoy," Laurence Sterne warned – to be healthy is to achieve the necessary foundation for life's other enjoyments. And for some, like Dr. Johnson, it's not only a prerequisite for happiness, it's an ethical imperative: "To preserve health is a moral and religious duty, for health is the basis of all social virtues. We can no longer be useful when we are not well."

A healthy body is a sexually-charged body. Immortal poetry and impeccable moral behavior and humanity-helping technological progress are all very fine, but the evidence would seem to indicate that nature put us here to eat, sleep, shit, and fuck. And, of course, make babies who will grow up to eat, sleep, shit, and fuck. Which was probably something like what Baudelaire was thinking when he wrote, "Sexuality is the lyricism of the masses." Baudelaire wasn't implying that the human body was shameful or that sex was dirty, only that sex seemed unworthy of the staggering devotion human beings so obviously pay it. If everyone does it, in other words, how can it possibly be worth doing?

Except, as Montaigne asked, "Is it not an error to consider some actions less worthy because they are necessary?" Maybe desires like the sexual impulse are creditable precisely because they *aren't* a decision. Perhaps obeying the dictates of nature is more of a virtue than complying with human-concocted imperatives. "What must first be proved is worth little," Nietzsche maintained. No one ever had to be convinced to be lustful. Lust commands, cajoles, and compels, even when – sometimes, especially when – one doesn't want to be lustful. Our awakened and aroused sexual organs are all the argument needed. Besides, as Cyril Connolly said, "No one was ever made wretched in a brothel [unless they have to work there]." Not while they were doing what they came there to do, anyway.

Then there is that other favourite thing one does while in bed: sleep. We shut our eyes so as to physiologically rest and rejuvenate, but sleep is also one of nature's kindest gifts, not least for its power of conferring the bliss of temporary forgetfulness. How often after "sleeping on it" do we arise to find a problem either diminished in intensity or solved, the mind busy working while consciousness is resting? ("Take rest," Ovid advises; "a field that has rested gives a bountiful crop.") Sometimes the best solution to a problem is to ignore it, and what stupor is sweeter than the oblivion of sleep?

As well, if Freud is correct and, aside from the sex drive, the death wish is what most deeply motivates human beings, sleep ("thou ape of death," as Shakespeare called it) is life's closest approximation to nonexistence, the sole human experience capable of replicating the soothing narcosis of nullity that the world-weary narrator of Swinburne's poem "The Garden of Proserpine" longs for:

I am tired of tears and laughter,
          And men that laugh and weep
Of what may come hereafter
          For men that sow to reap:
I am weary of days and hours,
Blown buds of barren flowers,
Desires and dreams and powers,
          And everything but sleep.

Besides, sleeping – or, more accurately, the delicious moments before unconsciousness engulfs one – is also simply physically, sensually, pleasurable. One of my fondest childhood memories is falling asleep buried deep underneath a delightfully heavy pile of mother-fussed blankets, the sudden low blast of the furnace promising five continuous minutes of wave after wave of grey-metal vent warmth. Even now, how pleasurable to have to get up to go to the cold bathroom in the middle of the night in the middle of winter because climbing back underneath the still-warm blankets is so wonderfully womb-like and welcoming.

And then there is the singular joy of napping. Naps physically revitalize, but there's also the psychological gratification that comes from doing what the majority of the rest of the world can only daydream about: stopping the clock in the middle of the busy day and turning one's back on industriousness and conscientiousness by pulling down the shade and peeling back the sheets and horizontally flouting all that one has been taught to think of as responsible and right. Henry Miller used to change into his pajamas every afternoon for his daily nap in ritualistic preparation for the spirit-soothing act a friend of his called putting "velvet in his vertebra." A nap is an invigorating middle-finger salute to a world that too often takes itself far, far too seriously.

But before one sleeps one first has to be awake, and, aside from post-coital drowsiness, there's no better natural sedative than hard physical exercise. Of course, the soporific effect of physical exertion is hardly its sole attraction. Everyone from our first physical-education teacher to Plato knew the overall life-enhancing value of regular physical exercise, the flood of endorphins alone it releases as soothing a mental salve as any over-the-counter mood enhancer. Which is why working out is fun, as good a reason to do anything as any. I played hockey and football and ran track as a pre-teen and teenager, but these days when I ride my exercise bicycle for thirty minutes followed by five minutes of dumbbell curls and sit-ups it's not about winning trophies or building self-esteem or impressing girls. Preventative healthcare benefits aside, it's about feeling good. Particularly when your profession is sedentary, it's pleasurable to feel your heart rate accelerate and your limbs and muscles stretch and your skin break into a good clean sweat. At my age there aren't any trophies to be won for climbing on my bike and dutifully doing my daily half an hour ride, but the happiness I experience while doing it and the hot shower I've earned afterward are rewarding enough.

More than one person has seemed surprised when they discover that the bike I ride every day is stationary. "Don't you want to go somewhere?" they ask. Headphones on and music blasting, my heart pounding, my blood pumping, my body perspiring, I'm already there. Besides, the world outside my front door still isn't the world I'm most comfortable with. I still, as O'Meara says, have issues with nature. This, in spite of our purchase two years ago of a cottage in the Haliburton Highlands.

I grew up in the suburbs and have lived in cities ever since I left home at nineteen. Mosquito bites and sopping humidity and cold wet feet and most of nature's ordinary sights, sounds, and smells still inconvenience me more than they amaze. A few years ago, however, I felt for the first time, whether out walking our dog through the trees and trails of High Park or sitting reading in the backyard underneath a shady tree on a hot day or watching the summer sky light with lightning, the tingling beginning of a desire for closer contact with nature. There was no illusion of incipient pastoral epiphanies or a naïve longing for a simpler, more rough and rustic lifestyle; only a feeling that I might be missing out on something, that a crucial pigment was lacking from my personal colour wheel.

What I envisioned is pretty much what happened: I work during the day in a small cabin overlooking the Irondale River that borders our property; I read in the evening in the screened-in sunroom to the sounds of crickets and frogs and river-splashing beaver; before I lock the doors and turn off the lights I take my final pee of the night outdoors under a black sky strewn with silver stars. It's unlikely I'll ever come to agree with Pope that "All are but parts of one stupendous Whole,/ Whose body Nature is, and God the soul," but I'm coming more and more to understand Voltaire when he says, "Men Argue, Nature acts." I've come to appreciate the solidity of nature and its indifference to the itchy ambiguities of human existence.

But rivers run dry and crickets and frogs die and the human body breaks down and one's sexual drive diminishes and the last sleep one takes is the longest. Even the heartiest humanistic optimist can't help but occasionally wonder if the undeniable pleasures of the material world aren't somehow compromised by their equally undeniable ephemerality. Montaigne certainly didn't think so:

> I, who boast of embracing the pleasures of life so assiduously and so particularly, find in them, when I look at them thus minutely, virtually nothing but wind. But what of it? We are all wind. And even the wind, more wisely than we, loves to make a noise and move about, and is content with its own functions, without wishing for stability and solidity, qualities that do not belong to it.

As with most of the big questions, I don't have any definitive answers. Or if I do, they're prone to change from one week to the next. Anyway, it's time for my workout. And I need to fill up the water cooler for when we leave for the cottage tomorrow. It's supposed to be warm and sunny all weekend with only a slight chance of rain on Sunday.

INDIVIDUALITY

Foremost we admire the outlaw with the strength of his convictions.

    —Robert Duncan

There's no age more conformist than youth, and my own was no different. If my parents couldn't afford to buy me high-top leather Nikes or Converse, I at least got to wear North Stars like everyone else whose parents blanched at paying more for running shoes than they did for a week's groceries. I wanted to grow up and play in the N.H.L.; I owned every Kiss record; I thought anyone who wasn't just like me and my friends was morally deserving of our collective derision; I thought the richest girls at my school with the expensive clothes and the long, clean, shiny hair the prettiest.

My first memory of wanting to appear different was wearing my toque in the summertime when I was nine or ten years old. Michael Nesmith, the actor/musician hired to play the "smart" Monkee on the half-hour television show of the same name (plural version), had been my inspiration. I don't know why I wanted to follow his fashion lead – probably to appear smart – but I did. I hadn't yet discovered, as Louis Kronenberger had observed, that "Individualism is rather like innocence; there must be something unconscious about it." No one thought I was smart. Mrs. Stull, the mother of one of my friends, thought quite the opposite, in fact – asked me if my mother knew I was wearing a wool hat when it was eighty degrees outside. When I said that she did, she told me to take it off anyway, at least while we were playing hot box, likely not wanting a neighbourhood kid suffering heat stroke or worse in her backyard.

High school is the age of willful eccentricity – the single most boring species of attempted individualism – a period when the obnoxiously insecure adolescent involuntarily sets about fulfilling Ambrose Bierce's definition of intentional oddity as set down in his *The Devil's Dictionary*: "ECCENTRICITY, n. A method of distinction so cheap that fools employ it to accentuate their incapacity." And this time the impetus is clear: a desperate, almost aggressive desire to separate oneself from everyone else – everyone else, that is, but those whom one is imitating. My personal formula for self-styled teenage authenticity was as follows: one part Jim Morrison's sneering sexiness; one part Jack Kerouac's self-destructive genius; one part Lou Reed's rock and roll misanthropy. If it turned out I was neither sexy, brilliant, nor genuinely pessimistic (impetuously pouty doesn't count), I could at least fall asleep at night on my waterbed (proud to be the only one in my grade thirteen class to have one) knowing that I'd cooked up a combination of personality traits to which no one else at Chatham Collegiate Institute knew the recipe. A failed invention is still an invention; the copyright, however useless, is still your own.

In retrospect one can at least semi-objectively distinguish the seeds of genuine individualism that were once-upon-a-time sown and why they were disseminated in the first place. Nietzsche – who evolved from aspiring Lutheran minister to dutiful, tenured philologist to modernity's outlaw Socrates – knew both who he didn't want to end up being and why, as well as how his own particular evolution of identity came about:

> [T]hey sit cool in the cool shade: in everything they want to be mere spectators, and they beware of sitting where the sun burns on the steps. Like those who stand in the street and gape at the people who pass by, they too wait and gape at the thoughts that others have thought . . . [Therefore] I moved from the house of the scholars and I even banged the door behind me. My soul sat hungry at their table too long; I am not, like them, trained to pursue knowledge as if it were nut-cracking. I love freedom and the air over the fresh earth; rather would I sleep on ox hides than on their decorums and respectabilities.

"Individuality is freedom lived," John Dos Passos wrote. Whether one's uniqueness can be translated into action – as it was with Nietzsche and the large, vital body of work he left behind – is individuality's best barometer. Not that anything exists *ex nihlio* – even the most earnestly eccentric personalities and the most unique works of art have their influences, however unrecognized at the time of impact or hazily perceived long after the fact. "Great poets seldom make bricks without straw," Ezra Pound wrote. "They pile up all the excellences they can beg, borrow or steal from their predecessors and contemporaries and then set their own inimitable light atop the mountain." Elsewhere Pound goes even further, claiming that the only immorality is to steal from inferior artists.

Thoreau noted that "We perceive and are affected by changes too subtle to be described," but along with these unavoidable, undetectable influences, Hemingway, for example, had the good sense to stylistically steal from Stephen Crane, Sherwood Anderson, and Gertrude Stein, while at the same time his work was also obviously influenced by his newspaper training, his war experiences, and even his father's suicide and his mother's domineering. Yet somehow his best work – his early work – sounds like nothing else and no one else's (the latter, far inferior books sounding like a parody of his earlier writing). And it's not only merely assimilating the right influences that contribute to the creation of something new and distinctive. "Generally speaking," the historian Carl Becker wrote, "men are influenced by books [or people or jobs or even their physical environment] which clarify their own thought, which express their own notions well, or which suggest to them ideas which their minds are already predisposed to accept."

This materialization of successfully internalized influences borders on the alchemical: without A, B, and C it wouldn't be possible to imagine D, yet D is something entirely unique and can only be understood on its own terms. Jonathan Richman and the Modern Lovers' "Roadrunner," for instance, is obviously derivative of the Velvet Underground's "Sister Ray" for its basic sound ("Roadrunner" employs essentially two chords – D and A, and only two bars of E – rather than "Sister Ray"'s three, but they share the same unrelenting, throbbing rhythm), but whereas "Sister Ray" is a paranoiac paean to certain big-city super-sleazes busy licking off someone's Pig Pen and searching for their mainline and not being able to hit it sideways, imploring someone else to whip it on me, Jim, whip it on me, Jim, "Roadrunner" is an urban ode of an all-together other sort, a celebration of late-night automobile travel with the radio on, and of the unacknowledged beauty of the modern urban environment, specifically the Boston suburbs. The introductory count-off itself ("One-two-three-four-five-six!") is a joyful announcement of what is to follow: unironic commemoration of the seemingly banal but ultimately beautiful, and an act of undistilled poetic observance. Jonathan Richman needed to worship Lou Reed and emulate Lou Reed so he could eventually become Jonathan Richman, the inimitable Jonathan Richman.

Underlying this entire argument, however, is the assumption that being or doing something unique is preferable to its obedient opposite. Certainly most people don't live or create as if this were the case, the numbing homogeneity of the day-to-day world (the same stale opinions, the same noxious habits, the same pedestrian pleasures) matched in its unrelenting uniformity by the monotony of the literary world in which I earn my living, where the same kinds of books continue to be written in the same kind of way and bought and applauded and forgotten by the same kind of readers ("Most prose writers [and readers] aren't even aware that the sentences they write [and read] have a sound," Alan Ginsberg observed, "are not even concerned with sound in prose . . . You wind up with an impersonal prose, a prose that doesn't proceed from anybody, and thus a kind of bureaucratic prose").

And even if someone does make the effort to live it or say it differently ("If I'm going to sing like someone else," Billie Holiday said, "then I don't need to sing at all"), it takes more than part-time passion to get the job done, as e.e. cummings knew when he wrote: "To be nobody but your-self in a world which is doing its best, night and day, to make you everybody else means to fight the hardest battle which any human being can fight; and never stop fighting." Thoreau claimed that "I would rather sit on a pumpkin, and have it all to myself, than to be crowded on a velvet cush-ion," but it's since been scientifically proven that long-term exposure of one's rear-end to pumpkins makes for a really sore ass. And everybody knows that if your ass hurts, your whole body hurts.

Gene Clark battled and fought – right up until he stopped fighting, giving in to exhaustion and heroin while criminally capitulating to L.A. record producers with funny ideas about how one of the era's finest singer-songwriter's music should sound in the wake of the career resurgence of the recently discofied Bee Gees. Sweet Gene Clark's songs can be rhapsodized over elsewhere, but it's enough for now to know that whether with the Byrds, Dillard & Clark, or on his own, nobody wrote grievy minor-key masterpiece melo-dies married to Rorschach test tell-tale lyrics that even came close. And even after every new album was praised by the right people and worshipped by the righter (those whose righteous worship counts most) and then, of course, died in the record stores and was soon after shipped back *en masse* to the cemetery warehouse, he just kept on keeping on, not enough space on each new record for all of the sparkling new Gene Clark gems he continued to unearth. Take the case of 1974's *No Other*, an album beautiful and brave at the same time (a tricky duet almost impossible to pull off) that thrilled approximately forty-seven people and for which he was rewarded by being dropped from his record label. Bereft of a recording contract (while Peter-fucking-Frampton was selling millions), playing 100-seat clubs (while his one-time colleagues were filling baseball stadiums and hockey rinks) without any record label tour support (a van, three men, their instruments, and thousands of midnight highway miles guaranteeing to generate just the right pitch of heat necessary to bring to a boil the usual cut-rate touring tedium, claustrophophia, and petty daily bullshit), Gene on acoustic guitar and harmonica along with a bass player and a lead guitarist spread the word whether the world wanted to hear it or not. Pick up *Live '75* (typically, not released until 2008) to hear how the Alamo was a nightly aesthetic experience for these three, and how they went down fighting every time with no illusions that anyone was coming to the rescue.

And no one ever did. You can bite steel, but you're just going to get spit on it. Gene Clark clamped down hard and held on for as long as he could, until one day his teeth shattered in his mouth and the piece of steel was still there and Gene Clark wasn't. Nietzsche wrote that "It has been said that misfortune sharpens our wits, but to the extent that it does so, it makes us worse; fortunately, it often dulls them." Fortunately, by the time his will began to weaken – one too many rich record company fool fooling with his musical future, one too many one-nighters followed by one too-many morning-afters, one too many reminders of how musicians with not even a quarter of his artistry could pay their rent on time and buy their kids birthday presents – he wasn't the same man he was before (nor, unfortunately, was his music the same), smack and booze and blown-out sycophants blunting the blow. Clark had obviously not read Irving Layton's poem "Advice for Two Young Poets:" "The idea's to drive *them* to madness and drink/ – not yourselves." Self-destruction may be understandable and even inevitable, but it's never venerable. Pity the poet with the skin-too-few, but don't deify him, at least not for that. Consider the case of Brian Wilson, the Beach Boys, and the non-recording of Wilson's projected masterpiece, *Smile*.

Once upon a time, whenever I felt like messing with people's minds when they were over at my house, I'd slip one of my *Smile* bootlegs into the stereo without announcing what we were going to listen to. It would never be long before "Do You Like Worms" or "I Love to Say Da Da" or "Vega-Tables" or one of several other songs that Brian Wilson and his hand-picked conspirator/lyricist, Van Dyke Parks, wrote and recorded for Brian's intended *magnum opus*, the never-released *Smile* album, elicited questions of "Who is this?" or, just as often, "*What* is this?" When I'd casually answer, "The Beach Boys," I almost always got the response I was after: "Not *the* Beach Boys." Yep, I'd reply, the very same.

The *VH 1-Behind the Music*-version of this story tells us that Brian Wilson was a pitiable victim, rock and roll's first Icarus, an amphetamine-fueled golden boy of AM radio who, in daring to aspire to create "a teenage symphony to God," flew just a little too close to the sun of pop music perfection and descended back to earth brain-charred and ego-shattered, never to fully recover. It's both a morality play for a culture that teaches that mediocrity and conformity are the

twin requisites for success and happiness, and an enthrall-
ing tragedy for those more Romantic sorts who believe that
simply being too sensitive qualifies as a noble aesthetic act.
And it's bullshit.

Smile was to be the musical culmination of everything
Brian Wilson had to offer to the world, a harmonically
beguiling, lyrically audacious, delightfully idiosyncratic,
madcap listening experience, leading Brian to boast to a
friend, "That's where I'm going and it's going to scare a lot
of people when I get there."

Unfortunately, the one who got scared most was Brian.
Brother Dennis' explanation for *Smile*'s abandonment and
Brian's consequent steady decline into an obese, house-
bound shell of the musical innovator he once was – "I think
it was the drugs" – is as appealing as it is brief, but it's certainly only fractional. The drugs, particularly acid, despu-
tols, and hash were definitely part of the equation – what
were once stimulating tools for creation soon becoming
debilitating impediments (fueling Brian's already legendary
perfectionism, for example, to the point that he was terrified
of releasing *Smile* for fear it wouldn't be good enough). Yet
greed – that most addictive of opiates – was as equally
destructive.

In the end, Capitol Records' incessant demand for new
Beach Boys product – *any* Beach Boys product – coupled
with Mike Love's (the same man who'd earlier admonished
Brian during the recording of *Pet Sounds*, "Don't fuck with
the formula, Brian") disparagement of both Brian's adven-
turous new musical direction and Van Dyke Parks' wittily
impressionistic lyrics (dismissing them as "acid alitera-
tion") eventually ate away at what little self-confidence and
resolve the speed didn't. The centerpiece of the brilliant,

shattered fragments that make up the cobbled-together version of the original *Smile* that fans like myself have acquired on the musical black market and via the thirty delectable minutes on disc two of the five CD *Good Vibrations* box set is "Surf's Up," a hauntingly melancholy, yet paradoxically stirring song that was intended to be nothing less than a deconstruction of the band's sun-in-the-fun image and a clearing of the deck for the sonic revolution to follow. The original demo is just Brian accompanying himself on piano. The Beach Boys themselves never ended up adding their vocals to the mix. Brian was too afraid they'd laugh.

But in spite of what most of Wilson's legions of apologists contend – those who see him purely as a too-sensitive gentle genius who was made a martyr to Art by all those nasty philistines who wiped his *Smile* from the face of rock and roll history – Wilson played his own pivotal role in the album's abandonment. If Mike Love acts the villain to Wilson's hero in the *Smile* tragedy, Brian is clearly a hero with a tragic flaw. The openness and childlikeness that helped him nurture his unique artistic vision was the psychic flipside of the damning vulnerability and maddening passivity that allowed calculating clowns like Mike Love to keep him from fulfilling his musical aspirations. "Ambition should be made of sterner stuff," Shakespeare wrote. When the folk purists in England booed Bob Dylan and the Hawks after he'd gone electric, Dylan didn't put down his Telecaster and sulk back to his bed in America, he shouted back. Loudly.

HUMOUR

The most completely lost of all days is that one in which one has not laughed.

—Catullus

We tend to find the writers we need at the precise moments we need them. As a twenty-two year-old recent university dropout spending my days loading transport trailers for $6.50 an hour instead of investigating the soundness of Kant's categorical imperative, I found Charles Bukowski's *Love is a Dog from Hell.*

What I needed at that time – and what Bukowski provided in abundance – was writing suffused with humour, swagger, and a bracing ribaldry, delivered in a simple but engaging voice, a *joie de vivre*-jolt to my academia-deadened spirit. Ultimately, an author *is* his or her voice, just like your friends aren't what they do for a living or who their parents are or the values they claim to have, but, rather, the sum of their personalities as one experiences them day after day, year after year. Bukowski's voice – jollily misanthropic, brayingly Romantic, proudly ill-mannered – became, for me, that of a spirit-tickling, soul-fortifying friend, one that I could count on for commiseration and encouragement after another long day at a lousy job I was lucky to have or after an even longer night wondering where the hell my life was headed.

"Common sense and a sense of humor are the same thing moving at different speeds," William James observed. "A sense of humor is just common sense, dancing." Bukowski's poems and prose were startlingly, refreshingly honest – so much literature that I'd read up to that point seemed affected and insincere by comparison – and they gleefully danced on the heads of pretension and solemnity, those twin enemies of good art and good times. As in his poem "doom and siesta time," where the narrator patiently listens to his death-fixated, physical-fitness-obsessed friend detail his new healthy lifestyle, only to remark to the reader

> but I don't want to pay
> all those gym fees.
>
> I go to bed
> with a liverwurst and
> onion sandwich at one p.m.
>
> After I eat I
> nap
> with the heli-
> copters and vultures
> circling over my
> sagging mattress.

Yep, I thought, that about sums life up. But how come no one else – especially those revered academic staples and CanLit must-reads – seemed to be saying it?

"Nothing is more curious," George Saintsbury wrote, "than the almost savage hostility that humour excites in those who lack it." Hostility and incomprehension. Until Mordecai Richler became a part of the Canadian mainstream – a *Maclean's*-worthy personality to whom one could point whenever we needed confirmation we had our own irascible but ultimately lovable folk heroes – he was routinely dismissed by that same mainstream as a writer of merely "funny books," an entertaining but ephemeral diversion on the literary landscape, and certainly not a *serious* writer of such eminence as, say, Marian Engel or Rudy Wiebe or Ethel Wilson. More than a simple case of it takes one to know one (although that's certainly part of it), an inability to accept that something can be both humorous and thematically significant is rooted in intellectual insecurity. Whenever unsure or unconfident about something, act as if you aren't. Act intelligent, in other words. Serious. Sombre. Sullen, even (because people given to weighty thoughts are often oppressed under the mass of their great intellectual burdens – just check out their pained author photos). The same goes for readers: boredom and tonal homogeneity is a small price to pay for knowing that one is a serious person because one is a reader of serious books. Laurence Sterne defined solemnity as "A mysterious carriage of the body, to cover the defects of the mind." Defects of the mind that directly impact the happiness of the life.

Francis Bacon claimed that "Imagination was given to man to compensate him for what he is not; a sense of

humour to console him for what he is." One of the greatest
gifts a sense of humour bestows is the ability to look
squarely at the truth – of oneself or of the world – and not
succumb to pessimism or despair, the equivalent of viewing an eclipse and not having one's retinas burned out. The
capacity to laugh at what is painful is an act of psychological shadow boxing, and without it we either avert our eyes
from life's less savoury experiences and facts or, as in the
case of most middlebrow art, merely squint at the sky and
hope that the sober expression on our faces compensates
for the superficiality of what we see and feel and have to
say.

Anthony Burgess was a very funny writer. In *A Clockwork Orange*, for example, he concerns himself with, among
other things, the free will versus behaviourism debate, the
appeal/repulsion of violence, and the human maturation
process, but nevertheless does so with a humorous touch –
not as a respite from his considerable concerns, but as a
means of helping the reader better experience and hence
understand the very same. His aesthetic – one might even
say epistemology – wasn't any different when writing
about the publishing history of *A Clockwork Orange*, and in
particular his annoyance at having the twenty-first and final, pivotal chapter of the novel ("Twenty-one is the sym-
bol of human maturity . . . Those twenty-one chapters were
important to me") deleted by his original American publisher. Compelled to cede to the publisher's demand for
truncation ("I needed money back in 1961, even the pit-
tance I was being offered as an advance"),

when Kubrick made his film [of *A Clockwork Orange*] –
though he made it in England – he followed the Amer-

ican version and, so it seemed to his audiences outside
America, ended the story somewhat prematurely. Audiences did not exactly clamour for their money back,
but they wondered why Kubrick left out the denoue-
ment. People wrote to me about this – indeed much of
my later life has been expended on Xeroxing state-
ments of intention and the frustration of intention –
while both Kubrick and my New York publisher
coolly bask in the rewards of their misdemeanour.
Life is, of course, terrible.

It's not, really – although it really can be: an undeniable
point of paradox Burgess makes delightfully, devastatingly
clear.

One doesn't have to write a novel or an essay about its
publication history to understand this – every day, people
employ this same survival skill in order to chuckle and cope
(as opposed to curse and capitulate). "The human race has
only one really effective weapon and that is laughter," Mark
Twain wrote. Humour provides us with perspective, never a
strength of *Homo sapiens*, especially if one has been drinking
a lot of coffee and it's four o'clock in the morning. "Humor,"
Christopher Morley conjectured, "is perhaps a sense of
intellectual perspective: an awareness that some things are
really important, others not; and that the two kinds are most
oddly jumbled in everyday affairs." When the explorer and
author William Beebe used to visit Theodore Roosevelt, they
would usually take an after-dinner stroll together. At some
point, one of them would initiate a customary ritual. Either
Beebe or Roosevelt would look up at the night sky and
remark something like, "That is the Spiral Galaxy of
Andromeda. It is as large as our Milky Way. It is one of a

hundred million galaxies. It is 750,000 light years away. It consists of one hundred billion suns, each larger than our sun." At that point silence would usually follow. Eventually, one of them would say, "Now I think we are small enough. Let's go to bed."

A pleasing consequence of the humility gained from humour's broad perspective is a tendency to undercut fundamentalism of all kinds: religious, political, moral. "I have never once in my life seen a fanatic with a sense of humor," Amos Oz observed in his aptly titled *How to Cure a Fanatic*. "[N]or have I ever seen a person with a sense of humor become a fanatic, unless he or she has lost that sense of humor." And this is because, Oz continues, "Humor contains the ability to laugh at ourselves. Humor is relativism, humor is the ability to see yourself as others may see you, humor is the capacity to realize that no matter how righteous you are and how terribly wronged you have been, there is a certain side of life that is always a bit funny." Milan Kundera claimed that he could tell if a person was an undercover member of the Czech Communist Party by whether or not they had a good sense of humour. I tend to use the same method when determining whether or not someone I meet might become a friend.

Humour also helps us recognize – and reconcile ourselves to – the absurdities of ordinary existence. My wife is an excellent driver – I've felt entirely safe with her behind the wheel while travelling through Arkansas flash floods, during L.A. freeway rush hour, and in the middle of Canadian blizzards – but if the car we're renting happens to have XM Radio and she insists, as she usually does, that I flip back and forth between the three all-comedy channels for some good stand-up, it's like driving with an epileptic using a strobe light to read the road map. One moment she's driving, smiling, occasionally laughing; the next – if the comic is good – she's overtaken by such literal eye-watering, stomach-clenching laughter that I worry we're going to swerve off the road.

Her favourite comics – and hence the most dangerous to our safety – are those who observe day-to-day life in a way which, once brought to light and considered from various angles by an intelligent, iconoclastic mind, turn out to be anything but simple or ordinary. It's humour's gift of the long view, but with the added benefit of allowing us to recognize something from our own lives, something that was there all along and that, unarticulated, we may have felt to be wonderful or horrible or maybe even a bit of both, but until the comedian brought it so forcefully to our attention, we never truly *understood*.

The Onion is an American satirical newspaper that parodies traditional newspaper editorials and routine Associated Press-style news stories. The key to its humor is presenting everyday events as newsworthy items, which they are, of course, if they're happening to you. As E.B. White observed, however, "Analyzing humor is like dissecting a frog. Few people are interested and the frog dies of it." Here's an excerpt from a fake news story published under the headline, *Local Teen Slated to Masturbate Furiously*, that is excruciatingly funny because it captures so well the painful agony of teenage male sexual adolescence:

SALEM, IN – In a move designed to relieve several years of pent-up sexual frustration, area teen Jeremy

Royce is slated for fever-pitched, white-hot masturbation later this evening.

The masturbation, during which Royce will bring himself to climax through the use of autoerotic manual stimulation, is hoped to provide Royce with a much-needed outlet for the carefully concealed state of sexual arousal in which Royce spends approximately 99.8 percent of his life.

Royce, a sophomore at Brushwood High School in nearby Cedar Creek, is at or near his sexual peak, but has thus far been denied access to the act of sexual coupling due to such socioeconomic factors as parental dependency, uneven adolescent facial complexion and lack of a car.

According to reports, tonight's experience promises to be particularly special. Carefully studying this month's HBO guide, Royce has noted that this evening's 3 a.m. movie promises "N, SSC," or Nudity and Strong Sexual Content. The film, the critically acclaimed *Atlantic City*, features Academy Award-winning actress Susan Sarandon briefly rubbing lemon juice on her nude breasts.

Said Royce, "Oh, man!"

In the end, though, what's most important about humour is that the friends I've had the longest remain my friends because we still laugh when we get together (and when we get together, laughing – and listening to music – is what we do most). My wife and I have been together for twenty years and have, thankfully, changed, both as individuals and as a couple, but we not only still laugh a lot – probably more, actually, since we see the world a little clearer now and so *need* to laugh more often – but we still laugh at the same daily irrationalities, absurdities, and inconsistencies. Just as one knows what a person's true (as opposed to merely espoused) values are by whom his or her enemies are, "Nothing shows a man's character," Goethe wrote, "more than what he laughs at."

Laughter is the loudest affirmation possible of our most deeply felt beliefs. "The earth laughs in flowers," Emerson wrote. So do we.

MEANING

Man – a being in search of meaning.
> —Plato

I get into trouble when I'm not immersed in meaningful work. When I'm not working on a book – a book I chose to write because it chose me to write it – my attention tends to wander, my body and my mind inevitably following suit. More than one writer has claimed that writing is easy, it's day-to-day life that's the hard part. And for me at least, the latter is hard because, as Shakespeare wrote, life is often "as tedious as a twice-told tale/ Vexing the dull ear of a drowsy man." Caring about something from first rising to last consciousness (even if not, of course, literally thinking about it the entire time) makes life interesting, or at least far less dull.

Without hockey (and the Detroit Red Wings, in particular), I believe that my father would die. Not metaphorically, but literally. When he underwent surgery for prostate cancer in the summer of 1996, I was less worried about the operation than with his recovery. When healthy, N.H.L.-less summertimes had always been survived with the help of hard yardwork and the kind of house repairs only possible in the warm weather months. This time, sentenced to a prolonged horizontal hiatus on the bed and couch, I was afraid that his boredom and restlessness would be compounded by all of the introspection-inducing extra time he'd suddenly be confronted with (this was a man, after all, who'd been working full-time since the age of thirteen and whose idea of relaxation is to wash our rental car). I knew he'd lost nearly fifteen anxiety-ridden pounds when first diagnosed with the disease, and I was afraid that being sentenced to sedentary weeks on end would impair his rehabilitation. Missing the exaltation of a Red Wing comeback victory and living without the thrill of a good, honest fight between two equally-matched men settling their disagreement with their sincere fists instead of their lying, middling mouths (unlike ordinary life), my father was saved, I believe, by the first World Cup of Hockey which took place early that September. Canada lost to the United States in the final round and we raged long-distance over the phone – I was living, at the time, with my wife in Texas – about the poor officiating, and we smouldered together over the smug American coach. I don't believe it's hyperbole to say that the rejuvenating distaste he felt for everyone but his team – our team – helped him recover. "If we have our own *why* of life," Nietzsche noted, "we shall get along with almost any *how*."

Clearly, the body doesn't lie, even when it comes to activities not revolving around a hockey rink such as reading. As an undergraduate encountering Nietzsche for the first time, this meant having to periodically set my copy of

Thus Spoke Zarathustra down and pace around my small room to avoid the danger of sentient over-stimulation. So many new ideas, insights, and observations in such rapid-fire succession, and such an underdeveloped brain – mine – to receive and process them, walking up and down the floor seemed the only sensible solution. The only antecedent to this had been my fortuitous high-school discovery of *The Portable Voltaire* at a second-hand furniture and knick-knack store. Lines like "This is the character of truth: it is of all time, it is for all men, it has only to show itself to be recognized, and one cannot argue against it" didn't send me marching around my parents' backyard, but they did help put me on the road to the University of Toronto and a degree in philosophy, even if the part about the superfluity of argumentation when the truth reveals itself turned out to be less real than ideal.

To be mentally moved to the point of a physical reaction disqualifies dilettantism and time-passing busy work, though – to be meaning-sated means to be absorbed, engrossed, even overwhelmed. It has to approximate what Paul Tillich meant by the state of "ultimate concern:" "an act of the total personality" that "claims ultimacy [in that] it demands the total surrender of him who accepts this claim" and "demands that all other concerns . . . be sacrificed." It's a joyful sacrifice, however, experientially akin to Paul Klee's gleeful depiction of how "Colour possesses me. I don't have to pursue it. It will possess me always, I know it. That is the meaning of this happy hour: colour and I are one. I am a painter." A painter, and a rapturously rapt happy human being as well.

Baudelaire, too, believed that a condition of captivating ultimate concern was what made existence most gratifying, and he wasn't particular about how this self-generated state of grace came about:

> Be always drunken. Nothing else matters: that is the only question. If you would not feel the horrible burden of Time weighing on your shoulders and crushing you to the earth, be drunken continually.
>
> Drunken with what? With wine, with poetry, or with virtue, as you will. But be drunken.
>
> And if sometimes, on the stairs of a palace, or on the green side of a ditch, or in the dreary solitude of your own room, you should awaken and the drunkenness be half or wholly slipped away from you, ask of the wind, or of the wave, or of the star, or of the bird, or of the clock, or whatever flies, or sighs, or rocks, or sings, or speaks, ask what hour it is; and the wind, wave, star, bird, clock, will answer you: "It is the hour to be drunken! Be drunken, if you would not be martyred slaves of Time; be drunken continually! With wine, with poetry, or with virtue, as you will."

It's hard to argue against drunkenness on Saturday night, but there is the matter of Sunday morning. Toxicity, for example, is oftentimes the unfortunate result when one too-dutifully follows the logic of *If a little feels good, a lot must feel even better.* Marlow in Conrad's *Heart of Darkness* – isolated and ostracized deep inside the jungle – understands the need for manufacturing meaning when none seems to exist, even if most people not similarly forsaken cannot:

You can't understand. How could you – with solid
pavement under your feet, surrounded by kind neighbours ready to cheer you or to fall on you, stepping
delicately between the butcher and the policeman, in
the holy terror of scandal and gallows and lunatic asy-
lums – how can you imagine what particular region of
the first ages a man's untrammeled feet may take him
into by the way of solitude – utter solitude without a
policeman – by the way of silence – utter silence,
where no warning voice of a kind neighbour can be
heard whispering of public opinion? These little
things make the difference. When they are gone you
must fall back upon your innate strength, upon your
own capacity for faithfulness, [when the] earth for us
is a place to live in, where we must put up with sights,
with sounds, with smells, too, by Jove! – breathe dead
hippo, so to speak, and not be contaminated. And
there, don't you see? Your strength comes in, the faith
in your ability for the digging of unostentatious holes
to bury the stuff in – your power of devotion, not to
yourself, but to an obscure, back-breaking business.

He also understands how Kurtz has gone too far in his
attempt to fortify himself against the enormity of nothingness that engulfs the Western mind marooned in the
meaning-drained jungle:

Ivory? I should think so. Heaps of it, stacks of it. The
old mud shanty was bursting with it. You would think
there was not a single tusk left either above or below
the ground in the whole country . . . You should have
heard him [Kurtz] say, "My ivory." Oh yes, I heard

him. "My intended, my ivory, my station, my river, my – " Everything belonged to him.

From the megalomania of the street-person preacher who believes himself Christ, to the systematic, murderous purges and mass starvations overseen by Stalin who believed his actions sanctified by his unswerving faith in the eventual dictatorship of the proletariat, the human hunger for meaning and resultant order can easily become ravenously ruinous. "One of the symptoms of an approaching nervous breakdown is the belief that one's work is terribly important," Bertrand Russell observed. Unfortunately, the insane rarely recognize their own insanity, usually either violently condemning or condescendingly pitying those who question the veracity (or even simple healthiness) of their fanatical faith. There's no one more annoying – or dangerous – than the recently converted.

It's not just the intensity of one's ardour that's potentially problematic, either – Baudelaire might have claimed that it's irrelevant whether it's wine, poetry, or virtue that spiritually sustains one, but, then, he never had to live in Toronto during the World Cup of Soccer. Two weeks of incessant flag waving and whistle blowing and horn blasting are sufficient testament to Dr. Johnson's assertion that "Patriotism is the last refuge of a scoundrel." We won; my country; God is on our side: all are admittedly spirit-sustaining props, but you weren't on the team and had nothing to do with them winning, the only reason you were born in country X is because your parents happened to fornicate there, and every country believes that God is on their side, just like every country is certain that they're the true guardians of freedom and decency and truth.

Prejudice may be, as William Hazlitt noted, "the child of ignorance," but its perennial plenteousness would seem to guarantee a fruitful and enduring existence. When my wife and I moved to southwest Texas to attend graduate school, my only significant experience with racial prejudice had been white on black (and vice versa) while briefly living, en route, in Wichita, Kansas. Living in Texas taught me that, lacking the usual (at least in the Unites States) prejudicial dynamic, human beings will simply find another unwarranted way to feel superior to one another (and hence feel better about themselves). Lacking a poor African-American community to look down upon, the poor whites simply derided the poor Mexican-Americans or, if necessary, the even poorer whites. "Passionate hatred can give meaning and purpose to an empty life," Eric Hoffer observed in his study of faith (religious and otherwise), *The True Believer*. It's no coincidence that the most virulent forms of race prejudice, like those of the Ku Klux Klan, are practiced primarily by the economically and socially marginalized who are bitterly oblivious of the conspiring economic and political forces that actually put (and keep) them there. "A hurtful act is the transference to others of the degradation which we bear in ourselves," Simone Weil maintained.

Even some of the more benign, if only slightly less demoralizing, patterns of human behavior can be traced to a deficiency of consciously-chosen, authentically-existing meaning. Victor Frankl believed that "striving to find a meaning in one's life is the primary motivational force in man." Unfortunately, "no instinct tells him what he has to do, and [increasingly] no tradition tells him what he ought to do; soon he will not know what he wants to do. More and more he will be governed by what others want him to do, thus increasingly falling prey to conformism." As a result, as Samuel Butler noted, you tend to end up with an epidemic of "People car[ing] more about being thought to have taste than about being either good, clever, or amiable." The infernos of excessive patriotism and ethical conventionality and conservatism in general always blaze brightest when fanned by the flames of social unrest or personal unease.

And yet we need it. We need to get drunk. Continually, if possible, as Baudelaire counseled. This, in spite of the fact that we know that intoxication is not our natural state and that in the morning we'll likely awake, ashen and unsteady, to sobriety. At least we *should* know. Because knowing that all of our spirit-nourishing beliefs and fervours are as ephemeral as the air we conjured them from is the best safeguard against the dangers of solipsism, self-importance, and fanaticism. Somehow maintaining this difficult, delicate balance – between passionately believing in something and courageously accepting this belief's ultimate transience – should be our goal, as Bertrand Russell advocates in his essay "A Free Man's Worship":

> That Man is the product of causes which had no prevision of the end they were achieving; that his origin, growth, his hopes and fears, his loves and his beliefs, are but the outcome of accidental collocations of atoms; that no fire, no heroism, no intensity of thought and feeling, can preserve an individual life beyond the grave; that all the labours of the ages, all the devotion, all the inspiration, all the noonday brightness of human genius, are destined to extinction in the vast death of the solar system, and that the whole temple of Man's achievement must inevitably be buried beneath

the debris of a universe in ruins – all these things, if not quite beyond dispute, are yet so nearly certain, that no philosophy which rejects them can hope to stand. Only within the scaffolding of these truths, only on the firm foundation of unyielding despair, can the soul's habitation henceforth be safely built.

Perfect – except for one thing. The foundation isn't firm and the house isn't safe. There *is* a foundation and the house *is* still standing, but it isn't made from the concrete blocks we wish it was and no one knows how long it will continue to remain upright. But it's the only house we've got, and some people aren't fortunate enough to have even that. Besides, so what if it's slightly ramshackle and maybe even near its ruin – it does have a certain undeniable charm, much like the house Edna St. Vincent Millay describes in her poem "Second Fig": "Safe upon the solid rock the ugly houses stand:/ Come and see my shining palace built upon the sand!" And after visiting, be sure to build your own. Winter is always coming, and the nights are always long.

FRIENDSHIP

Thank you, friends.

    —Alex Chilton

He was loyal – I can't count the number of times he judged me threatened and correspondingly responded in protectively cantankerous kind. He was a wonderfully agreeable companion – with only one other have I ever been able to work virtually side by side for hours without the slightest sense of self-consciousness or unease. Except for the very end when cruel cancer took him too soon, he was unfailingly affirmative, enthusiastic, and energetic. How could one ask for more from a friend? True, he always peed outside and he did like to roll in coyote dung when we'd walk in High Park, but one accepts one's friends as they are. Likewise, and to his considerable credit, he never said a word when I briefly took to wearing a buckskin vest in the early 1990s and always pretended he didn't notice any change in my hairline after I hit thirty.

Tennessee Williams admitted he'd never cried during a single performance of *Hamlet* or *King Lear*, but that even the most melodramatic B-film with a mistreated, apple-cheeked orphan could instantly bring him to tears. I'm the same, but with animals, particularly dogs, specifically the aforementioned, coyote-feces-rolling Barney and his still-very-much-alive successor, Henry. Part of this, of course, is unalloyed sentimentality, the uncontrollable reaction each of us has to self-evident offenses against what is so obviously good or right or innocent – the same manipulating force, incidentally, that powers all bad art. But it is also because most of the time I enjoy the company of dogs much more than I do that of humans.

A motel in the American South that my wife and I once stayed in had a sign hanging over the front desk that read: NO DRINKING, NO SMOKING, NO FIGHTING, NO CURSING, DOGS ALWAYS WELCOME. The sign, I think, was supposed to be funny – though three years of living in Texas taught me never to assume that anything you see or hear below the Mason-Dixon is intended to be obviously humorous or ironic – yet its underlying meaning couldn't have been more true. Dogs don't lie about their age to impress other dogs. Dogs don't talk too loud in public places on their cellphones. Dogs don't watch *American Idol* or read bestselling novels or buy Nickelback albums. Byron knew this, even if he lived two centuries too early to enjoy Alberta's most famous musical contribution to our fast-food culture. From his "Inscription on the Monument of a Newfoundland Dog":

> . . . the poor dog, in life the firmest friend,
> The first to welcome, the first to defend,

Whose honest heart is still his master's own,
Who labours, fights, lives, breathes for him alone,
Unhonour'd falls, unnoticed all his worth,
Denied in heaven the soul he held on earth:
While man, vain insect! hopes to be forgiven,
And claims himself a sole exclusive heaven.
Oh man! thou feeble tenant of an hour,
Debased by slavery, or corrupt by power,
Who knows thee well must quit thee with disgust,
Degraded mass of animated dust!
Thy love is lust, thy friendship all a cheat,
Thy smiles hypocrisy, thy words deceit!
By nature vile, ennobled but by name,
Each kindred brute might bid thee blush for shame.

But, the argument goes, although dogs might make for nice company and even supply a cheap, reliable source of furry home security, no dog ever wrote Shakespeare's plays, ever painted Monet's water lilies, ever composed Beethoven's symphonies. Occasionally, it must be admitted, human beings have put their opposable thumbs and weighty brain mass to good use. Whenever, for example, human greed, superficiality, or simple stupidity overwhelms me, making me want to fall down on all fours and resign my membership in all things *Homo sapiens*, I remind myself of the existence of the Beach Boy's *Pet Sounds* album. Any species capable of creating something as undeniably beautiful as "God Only Knows" can't be all bad. Sometimes we even treat one another well, exhibiting a moral talent not ordinarily utilized in our day-to-day dealings. More than sometimes, this uncommon magnanimity is directed toward another species, as the long-dead dog in Robinson

Jeffers' poem "The House Dog's Grave" knows well.

> I cannot lie by your fire as I used to do
> On the warm stone,
> Nor at the foot of your bed; no, all the nights through
> I lie alone.
>
> But your kind thought has laid me less than six feet
> Outside your window where firelight so often plays,
> And where you sit and read – and I fear often grieving for
>   me –
> Every night your lamplight lies on my place.
>
> I hope that when you are lying
> Under the ground like me your lives will appear
> As good and joyful as mine.
> No, dears, that's too much hope: you are not so well
>   cared for
> As I have been.

Though there are, naturally, exceptions, people do tend to treat their animal companions better than they do their human counterparts. It's not difficult to understand why. "Animals are such agreeable friends," George Eliot wrote. "They ask no questions, they pass no criticism." Dogs never think we're too old to play air-guitar in the middle of the afternoon with the windows shut and the stereo turned to eight. Dogs don't get disgusted with us when we decide to spend the evening slumped in front of the television instead of at the computer. Dogs never hint that maybe it's time to consider switching to light beer and taking out a gym membership.

It's not just our nimble fingers and fat brains that makes humans unique among other creatures; it is also our inexhaustible desire for things that we know we can never have. Things like physical immortality. Or moral or aesthetic perfection. Or unconditional love – this last chimera perhaps more than most. Real love is rare enough; the unqualified variety exists only in the parent-child bond, Idealistic philosophy, and bad Hollywood movies. With a single exception. And, as in John Updike's poem "Another Dog's Death," right until – faithfully until – the very end.

> She made her stiff legs trot and let her bent tail wag.
> We found a spot we liked, where the pines met the field.
> The sun warmed her fur as she dozed and I dug;
> > I carved her a safe space while she protected me.
>
> I measured her length with the shovel's long handle;
> she perked in amusement, and sniffed the heaped-up
> > earth.
> > Back down at the house, she seemed friskier,
> but gagged, eating. We called the vet a few days later.
>
> They were old friends. She held up a paw, and he
> injected a violet fluid. She swooned on the lawn;
> > we watched her breathing quickly slow and cease.
> In the wheelbarrow up to the hole, her fur took the sun.

Anyone who fails to understand why I'm still capable of tearing up when I recall Barney's dreadful last days or why, on our way to the cottage, I always appreciatively take off my hat when we pass the Newmarket O.S.P.C.A. – where we got Henry – is lacking not only an understanding of canines, but of friendship. It's not the number of legs that makes a friend.

Not that a few two-legged animals haven't made their own ample impression over the years. Eddie Webster was my first best friend. His mother was a friend of my mother's, so when Mrs. Webster came to visit when her husband and my father were working at the factory, Eddie usually came along too. It's one of my earliest memories: hiding underneath the kitchen table behind my mother's legs, and Eddie sliding across the gleaming clean, Pine Sol-fresh hardwood floor on his knees and asking, "Wanna play?" I always envied Eddie his superior bravado and vigour, which was likely the result of having two older brothers who set an exemplary unruly example and regularly employed him as a goalie-net target and all–purpose punching bag.

Sean was my first school friend, an African-American first-grader whose mother raised him and his sister by herself, and who either couldn't afford or be bothered to give him milk money. While the rest of us slurped our white or chocolate moo juice (I wanted chocolate, but my mother wouldn't hear of it), he stared out the window at the empty blacktop and pretended not to notice. Nothing about his life was as good as mine – I had more toys, better sports equipment, a mum *and* a dad – but Sean never seemed envious or upset and always appeared happy, always more appreciative when my mother put out milk and cookies for us when we were watching cartoons, or when my dad joined us outside to play catch.

Gary Bechard was next. Schoolyard foes and trusted teammates alike might have called him "Bubba" or "Fatman" or (our first lesson in irony) "Skinny," but Gary was a physical marvel and unwitting inspiration, our best offensive defensemen, a money-in-the-bank, jump-shot-shooting bowling ball of a point guard, and the rock-solid anchor of our medal-winning (you can look it up) boys 400 metre relay team. Eddie and Sean and Gary might have been the same age as I was, but they were all my teachers. "A man's growth is seen in the successive choirs of his friends," Emerson said. These three got me started, but the chorus was just warming up.

Jamie Dalzall was the first best friend that I had consciously wanted to be my best friend. He was good at sports, he was an honours student (this point could be overlooked), and he was equally popular with the jocks, the teachers, and the would-be stoners. Most of all, he was funny. He could imitate Tattoo and his boss Ricardo Montalban off of *Fantasy Island*, as well as the majority of our public school teachers. He came up with clever nicknames for other students (and once dubbed, say, "Chilly Willy," one *stayed* "Chilly Willy"). He'd not only discovered Monty Python on Saturday nights' ten p.m. PBS broadcast, he actually owned a handful of Monty Python albums that we would listen to over and over again, memorizing entire skits like "The Cheese Shop" and "The Undertaker," rendering the records themselves almost superfluous. Sharpening a nascent sense of humour; impersonating others; learning how to tell a story: who knew I was apprenticing to be a novelist? As far as I could tell, it was still a close call between growing up to be an R.C.M.P. officer or a N.H.L left winger who played it tough but who still had a nose for the net.

Jamie was the first friend I could be quiet with. It didn't seem like such a marvel of camaraderie at the time – we'd stand around drunk and alone together at parties in lieu of getting laid, or he'd borrow his parents' car and we'd go to Burger King after dinner on Sunday nights to use the two-for-one coupons we'd clip from the *Chatham Daily News*, and we'd sit in the car in the parking lot listening to WRIF and eating our Whoppers out of pure suburban teenage boredom – but time teaches that being able to avoid being alone while also being able to shut up (and having the other person shut up) is one of life's rarest delights. And as exceptional as shared silence is, Emerson noted another similar oddity of human amity when he wrote that "It is one of the blessings of old friends that you can afford to be stupid with them." Jamie watched me lose a fight to a bleacher at a high-school dance. He tolerated my shiny new earring. He witnessed me make a fool of myself for a girl who didn't merit it. "One loyal friend is worth ten thousand relatives," Euripides wrote. And the numerical odds of actually finding such a friend seems about the same.

University wasn't a time for me to join a frat or clubs or to go to all of the really cool parties (assuming I could find them and would be welcome inside). Everything I read in and out of class and everywhere I went and everything I saw in Toronto made me feel as if I was years behind where I wanted to be – *needed* to be – so human interaction wasn't as important as mingling with the best that has been thought and said (dead white European male and female variety). But if Abraham Maslow is right, and friendship ranks just behind such other essentials as food, water, and health (Edith Wharton went almost as far, claiming that "The only thing to do [in life] is to hug one's friends tight and do one's job"), it was inevitable that at some point I'd want to put down my book and pick up a beer and wish for someone to enjoy it with. I met Brad Smith in an Introduction to Moral

Philosophy class. The circumstances couldn't have been more apt.

Brad was, like me, a philosophy major, someone who understood Bach just as much as he did The Clash, but our real bond was drinking beer and being young. Together we shed our schoolboy shells and did our best to get into trouble in every wonderfully squalid bar and tavern along Queen Street West. What we mostly did was lean on each other as we stumbled in tandem toward adulthood. And maybe even more important than the troubles Brad listened to and the rants he endured was the assurance that he'd be there to listen and endure and even more if that was what I needed him to do. "It is not so much our friends' help that helps us as the confident knowledge that they will help us," Epicurus observed.

If, as Shakespeare wrote, "Most friendship is feigning, most loving mere folly," the chances of the two being successfully combined in the same person must border on the infinitesimal. Lucky, lucky me, then, that my wife is also my best friend (as well as, not surprisingly for a novelist, my first and best reader). When I'm unable to sleep with four a.m. anxiety, she's the one I wake up to help talk it away. When I'm happy with something I've done or experienced, she's the one I want to share it with, it somehow not feeling completely real until she has. When I don't want to be alone yet don't want the added burden of company, it's her I want to spend time with.

I ask a lot of her – to be my only lover, my best friend, my day-in, day-out companion. I ask her to be what Aristotle defined as a true friend: "one soul in two bodies." Maybe that's asking too much. The number of divorces and – even more depressingly – empty, merely functional relationships one witnesses seems to indicate as much. Perhaps Pascal had it right after all: "No one talks about us in our presence as he would in our absence. Human relations are only based on this mutual deception; and few friendships would survive if everyone knew what his friend said about him behind his back."

If that's the case, I just hope I don't hear what she has to say about me when she thinks I'm not around. Henry and I need her too much. I hope she needs us too.

SOLITUDE

In solitude, where we are least alone.

—Byron

Maybe I'm prejudiced – I *was* an only child; I never have felt comfortable at large dinner parties, political rallies, or group therapy sessions – but being alone has always seemed to me better than being with others. Not all of the time, obviously. "There are days," Colette wrote, "when solitude is a heady wine that intoxicates you with freedom, others when it is a bitter tonic, and still others when it is a poison that makes you beat your head against the wall." On days like these last we're fortunate to have friends who will help us keep our heads away from solid surfaces. But loneliness isn't the same as solitude. And a true friend would agree with Rilke: "I hold this to be the highest task for a bond between two people: that each protects the solitude of the other."

No matter how poor we were and no matter how small or shoddy the apartment or house we rented, my wife and I always insisted on each having our own workroom with a door that shut and locked. There's no human being whose company I enjoy more – there's no human being whose prolonged presence I can abide without having to resort to deep-breathing exercises – but, with Thoreau (although without the bucolic adjunct), "I think that I cannot preserve my health and spirits, unless I spend four hours a day at least – and it is commonly more than that – sauntering through the woods and over the hills and fields, absolutely free from all worldly engagements." I'm a better friend, husband, and citizen – more patient, more responsive, more sympathetic – when I've had ample time away from my friends, my wife, and my fellow citizens. Too long in the company of others and it feels as if my soul's oxygen supply has been siphoned off. *Contempt* may be too strong a word for what is bred from the over-familiarity endemic in everyday life (domestic or otherwise), but occasional irritation and exasperation certainly are not. The problem, as Thoreau saw it, is that

> Society is commonly too cheap. We meet at very short intervals, not having had time to acquire any new value for each other. We meet at meals three times a day, and give each other a new taste of that old musty cheese that we are. We have had to agree on a certain set of rules, called etiquette and politeness, to make this frequent meeting tolerable and that we need not come to open war. We meet at the post-office, and at the sociable, and about the fireside every night; we live thick and are in each other's way, and stumble

over one another, and I think that we thus lose some
respect for one another. Certainly less frequency would
suffice for all important and hearty communications.

Even though Thoreau has become a sort of patron saint
of the environmental movement (with minor saintly status
granted in civil disobedience), his core value lies in the independence of thought he both preached and practiced (a rare
combination). "It seemed as if his first instinct on hearing a
proposition," his friend Emerson said, "was to controvert it,
so impatient was he of the limitations of our daily thought."
Consequently, "no equal companion stood in affectionate
relations with one so pure and guileless. 'I love Henry,' said
one of his friends, 'but I cannot like him; and as for taking
his arm, I should as soon think of taking the arm of an
elm-tree.'" Nowhere did Thoreau diverge more vigorously
from popular opinion (then and now) than in his celebration
of solitude. Contrary to conventional wisdom, which
always argues for the compliant group member over the
self-reliant individual, Thoreau openly admitted that

> I find it wholesome to be alone the greater part of the
> time. To be in company, even with the best, is soon
> wearisome and dissipating. I love to be alone. I never
> found the companion that was so companionable as
> solitude. We are for the most part more lonely when
> we go abroad among men than when we stay in our
> chambers. A man thinking or working is always alone,
> let him be where he will. Solitude is not measured by
> the miles of space that intervene between a man and
> his fellows. The really diligent student in one of the
> crowded hives of Cambridge College is as solitary as a

dervish in the desert. The farmer can work alone in the field or the woods all day, hoeing or chopping, and not feel lonesome, because he is employed; but when he comes home at night he cannot sit down in a room alone, at the mercy of his thoughts, but must be where he can "see the folks," and recreate, and as he thinks remunerate himself for his day's solitude; and hence he wonders how the student can sit alone in the house all night and most of the day without ennui and "the blues"; but he does not realize that the student, though in the house, is still at work in *his* field, and chopping in *his* woods, as the farmer in his, and in turn seeks the same recreation and society that the latter does, though it may be a more condensed form of it.

Even when inclined toward solitude, resistance – especially when one is young – is often severe and relentless. Choosing to be alone means choosing not to be with those who don't – an implicit insult. Choosing to be alone means you're up to something secretive – an implicit threat. Choosing to be alone means you're selfish or anti-social or worse – an implicit sin. Nietzsche, another searing iconoclast with an elm-tree dinner-party demeanor, who it was probably preferable to get to know only a century after his death, discerned, "You crowd around your neighbor and have fine words for it. But I say unto you: your love of the neighbor is your bad love of yourselves. You flee to your neighbor from yourselves and would like to make a virtue out of that: but I see through your 'selflessness.'"

Granted that the compulsion toward escape from oneself (for whatever reasons) into the anonymous otherness of the other (whichever other) is all too-common at best, and existentially cowardly at worst, even Nietzsche acknowledged the difficulty of cultivating a "good love" of oneself (i.e., something beyond egoism or selfishness).

> One must learn to love oneself – thus I teach – with a wholesome and healthy love, so that one can bear to be with oneself and need not roam. Such roaming baptizes itself "love of the neighbor": with this phrase the best lies and hypocrisies have been perpetrated so far, and especially by such as were a grave burden for all the world . . . it is of all arts the subtlest, the most cunning, and the most patient.

Like happiness, one has to earn one's solitude.

"Man loves company, even if it is only that of a smouldering candle," the German aphorist Lichtenberg remarked. In addition, there has never been a lack of reasons to abandon the sometimes chilly isolation of solitary consciousness for the warm refuge of crowd consciousness: sundry psychological pains; unidentifiable but no less anguishing anxiety; indolence; boredom. Pascal argued that all human unhappiness can be traced back to the inability to sit alone quietly in one's room. His particular solution involved divesting oneself of the hair shirt of individual identity for the soothing anonymity of the Godhead. And certainly God, however defined, has long been one of human history's most ubiquitous means of eschewing private pain for collective calm – along with mass political movements, fervent, nearly religious nationalism, and any number of secular *isms* (most conspicuously in our time, consumerism). Humans always seem to find a way to flee their humanity.

And always there are new and even brighter flames to entice us. Even if moral progress has been hard to discern in this century and the last, technological advancements have been, even to a suspicious, near-Luddite such as myself, undeniably awe-inspiring. My grandfather was born into a world without telephones, cars, or air travel; the world he left behind upon his death outstrips even the most far-fetched science fiction of his boyhood. Humanity has literally achieved the unimaginable. Technology's most recent bequest has provided humans with the means to almost entirely obliterate enforced solitude. In the past, even those afraid or uncertain of the sometimes intimidating intensity of stillness and quiet were at least occasionally compelled to ride the bus alone or to sit quietly on the toilet with nothing or no one else for company but their own taciturn souls. Now, however, if there's no one to talk to on one's cellphone or no messages to listen to or no messages to text or to read or nothing online worth watching or worth Googling, there's always the reliable iPod ready to rescue oneself from any unwanted confrontation, however brief, with oneself. "Solitude is not something you must hope for in the future," Thomas Merton wrote. "Rather, it is a deepening of the present, and unless you look for it in the present you will never find it." Perpetually drunk with distraction, we're not becoming less knowledgeable – never have so many people had such easy access to so much information – just less human. And a head full of facts has never been a prerequisite for being wise.

Busyness is the antithesis of creativity: the former is energetic but empty, the latter typically protracted but enduring. "The greatest events," Nietzsche claimed " – they are not our loudest but our stillest hours. Not around the inventors of new noise, but around the inventors of new values does the world revolve; it revolves inaudibly." Most of the men and women I look to as heroes rarely ventured far from their secluded worlds, seldom counted more than a handful of people as friends, and were frequently clueless as to what the busy world outside their doors was up to. Their characteristic isolationism and quietism I've never viewed as anything but vigorous and fierce.

In attempting to draw up a blueprint of the prototypical, solitarily dedicated fiction writer, one could do far worse than to plagiarize the real life of American novelist and short-story writer Richard Yates. Alcoholic; subject to destructive bouts of mental illness; frequently destitute; crippingly self-obsessed; raised by an eccentric mother he loved and (mostly) loathed and haunted by a nondescript father he hardly knew; a trial to even his closest, most loyal friends – Yates' life seems almost a pathetic confirmation of every writerly cliché. Yates even smoked too much – a four-pack a day man for over forty years – and, at the time of his death, most of his books were either out of print or forgotten by everyone but a rarefied contingent of readers.

On the other hand, Yates was that most uncommon thing among artists: impatient – and often openly hostile – to pretension wherever he found it, whether it be aesthetic or personal, and disdainful of the sort of social networking and mutual back-scratching that contributes at least as much to a successful writing career as talent and perseverance. He was, above everything else, a supremely devoted craftsman who, quite literally, gave his life for his art.

Here's Andre Dubus on Yates' apartment (a place not unlike that described by Yates' biographer Blake Bailey, with its "bloodstains on his desk chair cushion (from piles), the calm roaches in plain sight, nothing but bourbon and instant coffee in the tiny kitchen"): "It was, I believed . . . a place young writers should be able to go to, and sit in, and ask themselves whether or not their commitment to writing had enough heart to live, thirty years later, as Dick did; with time his only luxury, and absolute honesty one of his few rewards."

W.B. Yeats wrote that "the intellect of man is forced to choose/ perfection of the life, or of the work." Richard Yates made his choice. Quietly. Behind four walls. Alone.

But it all comes back to happiness, the only litmus test that truly matters. The alcoholism and the pathological smoking and the mental illness notwithstanding – and regardless of whether or not the suffered-for books are any good or will be read – Yates was undeniably happier when alone and working than when not alone and not working. "Nowhere can man find a quieter or more untroubled retreat than in his own soul," Marcus Aurelius wrote. Maybe not quite as quiet as we'd like or as untroubled as we'd prefer, but better, anyway, than the more convivial alternative.

What many of *Walden*'s admittedly sincere admirers fail to understand is that rural escapism wasn't Thoreau's fundamental message; this is why, even though the vast majority of North Americans now live in cities and "nature" is increasingly only something that the relatively well-off can afford to "get back to," Thoreau remains more relevant than ever. Our present political and economic masters have learned well from the mistakes of their predecessors – the best way to enslave us is to have *us* be the ones to slip on our chains and keep strict guard over ourselves. Reading and watching the same news and listening to the same music and thinking the same thoughts and buying the same products, we do the job of jailer better than any soldier could, our gleefully blunted and acquiescent minds the perfect omnipresent censor. What Thoreau truly venerated was independence of thought and its twin virtue of nurtured solitude – the hallmarks of a civilized and free mind.

"The happiest of all lives is a busy solitude," Voltaire wrote. I think of my father cutting the grass and pruning the bushes and uprooting weeds in the backyard, for hours silently and expertly going about his business, occasionally humming a tune he can't remember the name of. I think of my mother inside the house doing her best on two arthritic knees to vacuum a carpet that doesn't really need vacuuming, with a load of clean dishes in the dishwasher ready to be put away once she's done. I think they're happy.

THE CRITICAL MIND

The one thing in the world, of value, is the active soul.
　　—Ralph Waldo Emerson

Covering virtually one entire side of the four-drawer filing cabinet in the room where I write is my wall of
heroes – a collage of pictures of people who have inspired
and continue to sustain me. For anyone who knows either
me or my work, the choices aren't surprising: Mordecai
Richler, Emily Dickinson, Thomas McGuane; Gram Parsons,
Ronnie Lane, John Hartford; old friends, deceased pets,
favourite relatives. Portraits are rarely removed because
earning a spot in the first place is equally rare. Additions are
occasionally made, although it usually takes my wife awhile
to notice. Not long ago, she did.

"Who's the fatty?" she said.

My wife lacks pretension to an extraordinary degree,
useful in a partner when your profession – the making and

selling of literature – is as thick with it as lung disease among miners.

"Edmund Wilson," I said. And just for the record, he wasn't always fat; was, in fact, nearly as nattily trim as Scott Fitzgerald when both were undergraduates together at Princeton. One tends to get a little defensive about one's Gods.

"Why is he up there?"

"Because he's a great man."

"Why, though? What makes him so great?"

An elemental, and therefore excellent, question.

Wilson's is the only photograph on my filing cabinet whose subject is a literary critic, admittedly not the sexiest career path one can pursue. Wilson's deepest instinct, unlike friends such as Fitzgerald and Edna St. Vincent Millay, was always for understanding, not creating. While he wrote entertaining light verse and passable fiction and plays, and he was an obsessive diary keeper – his always clean, crackling prose illustrating his sure feel for language – Wilson's truest talent was for criticism (although the poverty of contemporary connotations of that word do an injustice to Wilson's considerable gifts). Wilson recalled saying to himself when he was seventeen, "I am a poet," then – pausing, clarifying, correcting – "No: I am not quite a poet, but I am something of the kind." The pause is what is truly prescient.

Every critic – every writer – is what they bibliographically eat, particularly when they're formatively hungriest – when they're young – and Wilson's diet was not only extraordinarily fortifying, but, for a future critic, uncommonly varied. A solid scholastic grounding in Greek and Latin imbued a passion for both the ideal of classical objectivity and what Gore Vidal calls "the long view," and his mentor Christian Gauss' lectures at Princeton were extremely influential as well, not only for their then novel study of non-English literature but in conveying, via Gauss' own convincing example, that one must be loyal to the truth no matter where it led or who it hurt. (More than one long-term friendship was strained – some beyond repair, as with Nabokov – as a result of Wilson's unwillingness to pull his critical punches.) The obvious early-twentieth century critical touchstones were also important to Wilson – super-scoffers of modern maladies such as Mencken and Shaw – but maybe most influential were the nineteenth-century humanistic literary critics (whom the New Critics disparaged as "Impressionists") such as Arnold, Saint-Beuve, and Saintsbury: men who saw their primary responsibility as compelling others to love what they loved.

Wilson was the son of a Princeton and Columbia-educated lawyer, a man whose tools of trade his son described as "learning, logic, and dramatic imagination and eloquence," the very same tools Wilson would employ over the course of fifty years of elucidating, advocating, and exposing the books and ideas (good, bad, and inconsequential) of his time. A literature-as-subject-of-study autodidact, I – among many others – owe a great debt to Wilson for not only consistently steering me in the right aesthetic direction, but also for helping to develop my own critical sensibility. Give a person a good book, he'll have something to read for a week; teach a person how to critically separate the wheat from the chaff, and you provide him with the skills to read well for the rest of his life. Note: *read* – not *study*. The most valuable result of the finely tuned critical mind turned toward the world of books is assisting the common reader in reading – and therefore living – better. "Reading," Bacon reminds us, "maketh a full man."

Virginia Woolf liked this idea enough to entitle a collection of essays *The Common Reader*, quoting with approval Dr. Johnson: "I rejoice to concur with the common reader; for by the common sense of readers, uncorrupted by literary prejudices, after all the refinements of subtlety and the dogmatism of learning, must be generally decided all claim to poetical honours." Common sense not, unfortunately, all that common, particularly today when a literary reputation is more often than not the result of a lavish publicity campaign and maintained, if at all, by academic appropriation. At the time of his death, for example, most of F. Scott Fitzgerald's books were no longer in print; now, it is a rare American high-school or university student who manages to escape being forced to read *The Great Gatsby*. It's difficult to decide which scenario is more depressing.

Alfred Kazin's picture isn't on my filing cabinet, but he was a fine critic in the late, lamented tradition of Wilson, Woolf, and other intellectuals without tenure, free-ranging thinkers who read, wrote, and published outside academia. Kazin liked to identify himself as a life-long "private reader" – another name for that endangered species Gore Vidal identified as "voluntary readers" – the sort of person who reads *Ulysses* because he's curious to understand how Joyce changed the way the twentieth-century novel was to be conceived, and not simply because it's on a graduate-school course syllabus. The critic, for Kazin, didn't exist for the sake of other critics, but for other common readers.

> [W]hat I look for in a critic is his use to me; I can use critics whose general point of view is outra-

geous to me, but who in specific matters have this capacity for making a writer real and a text real . . . Criticism exists, after all, because the critic has an intense and meaningful experience of a work. And if he doesn't, why pretend that he does? Why bother, if what one is doing is not intensely real to oneself?

If anything, Kazin's admirably busy brain sometimes got in the way. Writing of the rise and fall of the poet Delmore Schwartz, for example, Kazin concluded that Schwartz "was hopelessly caught up in a logical web [and] was a terrifying and terrified rationalist, a prisoner of his superb intellectual training." All of which might have been true, but which entirely ignores the not insignificant fact that Schwartz was also a Benzedrine-addicted alcoholic whose poisoned body was as responsible for his decaying art and early death as his reason-manacled mind. A library isn't the only place one can learn about human nature. And books are not the only place one's mind can – and should – be applied critically. There is also what Stephen Dedalus in *Ulysses* dubbed the nightmare from which he was trying to awake: history.

Until relatively recently – September 11, 2001, to be precise – most North Americans not old enough to remember Pearl Harbor would likely have had as much difficulty comprehending Stephen's lament as they did the novel from which it came. To them – to most of us, that is – history has always been something that happened over *there* to *other* people, something that we, happily cocooned on our cozy continent of steady technological progress and world-envious wealth, might observe on television or read about in the newspaper and occasionally *tsk tsk* over. But not any-more. History has finally come home.

At the very least, it's undeniably invigorating to be a part of the game again after so many dull, delusional decades of sitting smugly on the sidelines merely keeping score and emitting the occasional cheer (South Africa's free-dom, the fall of the Berlin Wall) or boo (Soviet tanks rolling into Czechoslovakia, Pol Pot's horrors). Or, for instance, and much more recently, whereas it was always fascinating to learn about McCarthyism and marvel at how silly all those Red-hating Republican-types were way back there in the Middle Ages of the 1950s, it is chilling – and yet, somehow, also fascinating – to see the same insidious censoriousness occuring today in our freedom-smothering, Uncle-Sam-organized world, where if you're not firmly in favour of American Imperialism there's a good chance that your record albums will be burned or at least banned from the airwaves, employment opportunities will shrink and even disappear, and you'll run the risk of being labeled a terrorist, a rogue state, or whatever other term it is that the bad guys are going by this week.

But one doesn't have to be a super-savvy intellect like Noam Chomsky or an actual eye-witness to the horrors being perpetrated in Iraq in the name of cheap oil to think more clearly and correctly about the world outside one's window. George Orwell wrote many uncommonly sensible things, probably none more so than "the worst thing one can do with words is to surrender to them." Because, unlike Orwell's, our evil is thermal nuclear, multi-national, and usually accompanied by its very own soundtrack when it appears on CNN, we tend to believe that the source of our post-modernist political sorrows is anything but tied up with matters merely linguistic. Wrong. In the beginning is always the word.

If one were to read, watch, and listen to only mainstream, corporate-controlled media, for example – which, of course, the majority of any population always does – the United States' invasion of Iraq is not only understandable, but laudable. For one thing, it's implicit that it's not an *invasion*, it's a *war*, a crucial distinction. The Americans, it would seem, are only defending their country – and, by their munificence, all other freedom-loving countries – with pre-emptive strikes against the recent rise of world terrorism.

Spin the bottle of Babel, however, and you'll often get a very different understanding of who hit who first and who was only striking back. If, for instance, we define terrorism as Jonathan Barker does in his straight-forwardly sensible *No-Nonsense Guide to Terrorism*, as having three central elements – "violence threatened or employed; against civilian targets; for political objectives" – the popular image (in North America, at least) of a terrorist as a crazed fundamentalist (usually dark-skinned and religious) is significantly altered, expanded, and necessarily reconsidered. Reasoning like this – reasoning one obviously isn't going to read in the *National Post* or see on Fox News – helps to answer the question that George Bush infamously asked and that the majority of American citizens silently and sometimes not so silently (e.g., the Midwestern diner owner who changed the name of "French fries" on his menu to "freedom fries" to protest the French government's inexplicable refusal to join the American-led attack on Iraq) wonder: "Why do they hate us, when we're so good?"

To what end, though? "All that is necessary for the triumph of evil is that good men do nothing," Edmund Burke said. But dutifully applying one's critical skills to the political arena won't keep people from dying for the sake of discounted gasoline prices or stop the environmental suicide human beings seem so determined to commit any more than good critics will ever stop the majority of people from reading and praising bad books. Ultimately, as Seneca observed, it would seem that "One has to accept life on the same terms as the public baths, or crowds, or travel. Things will get thrown at you and things will hit you." But at least one will know why and by whom and even, if one is especially cunning, when to duck.

I'm glad that Edmund Wilson and Alfred Kazin and Virginia Woolf and Noam Chomsky and Jane Jacobs and Rachel Carson and Gore Vidal and Edward Abbey and many others have taught me how to read better and think clearer and understand more. More than that. I'm grateful.

PRAISE

No one suspects the days to be gods.

—Emerson

An interviewer once asked me if I considered myself a satirical novelist. I replied something to the effect that if one is even partially conscious one can't help *but* be satirical, novelist or not. "Against stupidity the Gods themselves contend in vain," Schiller wrote, and he never had to listen to one pimped-out politician or media-puppet dismiss global warming as a liberal fabrication, or risk channel-hopping across a single episode of *Dancing with the Stars.* Besides, ridicule has its health benefits, the daily disparagement of this or that worldly absurdity a swift and easy way to keep one's wit quick and one's blood bubbling warm.

Yet, blame, as Emerson wrote, "is safer than praise," and anything as culturally pervasive as the shallow cynicism that permeates even the most mediocre entertainment product passed off as cutting-edge culture would seem to indicate that rolling one's eyes is not the spirited exercise one's flabby soul so obviously needs. Meanwhile, "Irony scratches her tired ass," Jim Harrison has said, with the tired result too often being that focusing on the shallow and inconsequential tends to make oneself shallow and inconsequential.

More significantly, if not quite a compulsion, there exists at least a tendency or a tug in the other direction in the human psyche – away from cynicism and castigation, in other words – toward affirmation and celebration. Too much time in the skeptical shade necessitates an interval of reviving light. Nietzsche, *contra* his usual identification as either the father of modern nihilism or as the gleeful bearer of the bad news that God is dead, was fervently concerned throughout his work with the human need to affirm and even to exult. "Esteeming itself is of all things the esteemable treasure," he wrote. "Through esteeming alone is there value: and without esteeming, the nut of existence would be hollow."

When I met my wife Mara, I was a frustrated philosophy student looking for a way to bend the department's fairly conservative curriculum toward what I wanted to study – namely, the big questions of existence that the majority of my analytically-inclined professors weren't so big on, things like why we're here and what's good and bad and what's beautiful and what isn't. I thought I'd found a way around this academic impasse when I discovered the work of such psychic explorers as the psychologists Abraham Maslow and Eric Fromm, academically-approved professor types, but with a more open attitude toward the quasi-spiritual questions I was interested in. I remember handing her a copy of a recent revelation, Maslow's *Religions, Values and Peak-Experiences*, a book that explored how, once basic human needs like food, sex, and security were fulfilled, moments of extraordinary experience, known as "peak experiences," were possible (and possible to academically study), profound moments of love, understanding, happiness, or rapture, during which a person feels more whole, alive, and self-sufficient. She flipped through the paperback and read a paragraph or two before pronouncing, "It seems picky, doesn't it?"

Picky? *Picky*? I saw outlaw philosophy and she saw picky? Later, after she got me reading e.e. cummings, her favourite poet at the time, a line of his helped me see what she already had: "I'd rather learn from one bird how to sing than to teach ten thousand stars how not to dance." Why merely classify peak experiences, in other words, when one can actively cultivate them oneself or assist others in doing so, as a poet or a musician does? Or a novelist, for that matter. Instead of learning how to become a better scholarly classifier and footnoter, I commenced learning how to become a better dancer. "You higher men," Nietzsche wrote,

the worst about you is that all of you have not learned to dance as one must dance – dancing away from yourselves! What does it matter that you are failures? How much is still possible! So *learn* to laugh away from yourselves! Lift up your hearts, you good dancers, high, higher! And do not forget good laughter. This crown of him who laughs, this rose-wreath crown: to you, my brothers, I throw this crown. Laughter I have pronounced holy; you higher men, *learn* to laugh!

Dancing, laughing, affirming: nice work if you can get it. But there are some occupational hazards: most troublingly, as theologian Harvey Cox put it, the difficulty of

> reconcil[ing] a high degree of critical self-consciousness with a burning desire for experience [what Cox elsewhere calls "joyful immediacy"], which is not spoiled by too much self-analysis ... Religious language [such as praise, affirmation, worship] including the word 'God' will make sense again only when the lost experiences to which such words point become a felt part of the human reality. If God returns we may have to meet him first in the dance before we can define him in the doctrine.

So now we're back to Nietzsche and his desire for us to learn to dance, to learn to rush toward existence and embrace it (both the good *and* the bad) and even celebrate it.

To praise means not settling for second-hand, pseudo-experiences. The predilection is both inbred (it's easier) and institutional, as when one is culturally encouraged to dutifully click one's digital camera rather than to intently and openly look at that which one is taking a picture. It's easier to say "I was there" (with a photograph to prove it) than to understand where one was and what the experience actually meant, but it's not the same as living. Or, at least, it's not the same as living well.

To praise means to pay attention. Paying attention can be enlivening and exhilarating, but also arduous and exhausting. To love a work of art, for example, demands that the object of one's ardour be intimately and intensely known, like a lover. To read well is nearly as hard-won an art form as it is to write well. Nabokov described the good reader as having both "a poet's patience and scholiastic passion" for handling details.

Walt Whitman claimed that to have great writers, we need great readers. I've always thought it would be a sound investment in Canadian culture if all of the branches of government that are in the business of handing out grants to writers also awarded endowments to as many readers as possible, the stipulation being that, instead of gobbling down this season's must-read multi-generational saga of memory, loss, and heart-warming forgiveness, a strict regimentation of reading good books under the guidance of good teachers be undertaken, with the condition that, in the end, if the recipient still cannot discern the qualitative difference between the prose style of, say, Wally Lamb and Walker Percy, the grant would have to be paid back in full, with interest.

For the poet and critic Al Alvarez, true appreciation of a work of literature is "not about [gleaning] information, although you may gather information along the way. It's not about storytelling, although sometimes that is one of its greatest pleasures." It's about listening to a voice "unlike any other voice you have ever heard and it is speaking directly to you, communing with you in private, right in your ear, and in its own distinctive way."

Real writers, like one's real friends, don't quite sound like anyone else: they can only be who they inimitably are, their single most praiseworthy quality. The reason so many people are so boring is because they all tend to sound the same. The same, sadly, can be said for much of what masquerades as literature. Alvarez contends that "finding your own voice as a writer [or your own ear as a reader] means – or is the equivalent of – feeling free in your own skin. It is a great liberation. Yet the only way to achieve it is through minute – the minutest – attention to detail."

Paradoxical, yes, but absolutely true. When a fan asked Britain's greatest electric guitar player, Richard Thompson, the secret to his always innovative playing, Thompson's response was as sobering as it was succinct: "Practice your scales." What this means for the reader in search of genuine communion with a work of literature is that he or she must learn to "listen . . . as attentively as the writer writes," as Alvarez maintains, "hearing the tones and overtones and changes of pitch, as absorbed and alert as if he and the writer were in conversation together."

To experience something (a book, another person, a moment) wholly, however – for something's holiness to be experienced – means that participation is only the first necessary step toward eventual cogitation. What is experienced needs to be articulated. This is why celebration without stirring, deeply felt ritual (gluttonous Thanksgiving dinners bereft of genuine thankfulness, for example) rings hollow: we need to understand and declare (if only to ourselves, as in prayer) what we're celebrating. We need the right words, the appropriate language, if we are to achieve Cox's "joyful immediacy." Nearly two hundred years ago Shelley claimed that, in spite of humanity increasingly taking its orders from science and consequently relegating concern for the precise use of language to such quaint customs as sun worship and bloodletting, poetry (by which he simply meant the conscientious and dexterous manipulation of language) wasn't, in fact, a cultural anachronism, but, instead, the bedrock of any life worth living. Poetry, he claimed, defeats the curse which binds us to be subjected to the accident of surrounding impressions . . . It makes us the inhabitants of a world to which the familiar world is a chaos . . . It . . . purges from our inward sight the film of familiarity which obscures from us the wonder of our being . . . It creates anew the universe, after it has been annihilated in our minds by the recurrence of impressions blunted by reiteration.

The first time she said she loved you the skies opened up and a hundred violins provided the soundtrack in your head; 1001 times later, when she calls to say, "Can you pick up milk and bread on the way home from work tonight, thanks, I love you," it doesn't mean she loves you less: very likely she loves you more, and certainly more deeply. What it means is that the word "love" has slowly been drained of its meaning due to repetition and overexposure and wanton misuse. Consequently, a new word or words are needed. "Take a commonplace," Jean Cocteau wrote, "clean and polish it, light it so that it produces the same effect of youth and freshness and spontaneity as it did originally, and you have done a poet's job."

I've rarely given in to the temptation to see the musical artists I admire – when they were young, on record – imitate themselves on stage when they're old. A large part of Jerry Lee Lewis' genius, for instance, was in the animalistic anarchism of his performances (whether live or recorded); to go and watch him as an infirm old man plod through rote remembrances of teenage paeans to lust and heartbreak borders on the sacrilegious. Better to stay home and listen to the records and look at the pictures on the back of the LPs taken when the Killer was still the Killer.

A few years ago, however, a confluence of mostly non-musical factors – the need for a quick and relatively cheap vacation while our kitchen was being renovated; the sudden availability of tickets; the promise of a smaller than usual venue – led my wife and me to Niagara Falls to see Bob Dylan in concert. We arrived a day early to view the sights – I hadn't been to the Falls since I was a child – and, after being appropriately appalled by the neon and concrete boob job that had been given to one of nature's eight wonders, we went looking for the site of the next night's concert. And for some reason we couldn't understand (or believe), Dylan, it transpired, would be playing in an outdoor location no bigger than the size of half a football field. Because you could only buy tickets for the show through the hotel – which you needed to stay at in order to qualify for ticket purchase – we reconciled ourselves to the fact that we'd probably been duped and comforted ourselves with the thought that at least the last coat of stain on the hardwood floor would be dry by the time we got home.

The next night we stood in line for half an hour or so outside the advertised venue – the grounds, it turned out, were owned by the hotel and were used for large wedding parties and the like – and came to the conclusion that our tickets, which advertised BOB DYLAN and BAND, were likely a misprint and that what we'd really paid to see was probably Bob Dylan's back-up band. We sipped from our plastic cups of foamy beer and stood with perhaps three hundred other people in the warm evening, and watched as Bob Dylan walked out on stage. A wrinkled, stooped, slightly befuddled-looking Bob Dylan, but Bob Dylan nonetheless. Though we were already only thirty feet from the stage, my wife lifted up a red rope intended to safeguard the hotel's VIPs, and we slipped underneath and took our place ten feet from the stage. Ten feet from Bob Dylan on the stage.

Musically, the show was irrelevant, a croaking, barely-singing Dylan basically performing Bob Dylan karaoke backed by a band of bored professionals. If Bob Dylan feels the need to unceasingly travel the world impersonating himself on stage every night, then that's what Bob Dylan should do, he's earned the right to artistic irrelevancy. But I was standing ten feet away from someone who'd not only changed my life, but someone who'd had as much impact on twentieth-century culture as Picasso or Charlie Parker or Hemingway. I watched him clear his throat between songs and spit a gob of something more solid than liquid to the left of his keyboard. I'd just watched Bob Dylan hork.

Later, after the show, two things happened – or, rather, didn't. First, I couldn't get drunk, and not just because of the obscenely expensive bottles of Heineken for sale at the local plastic nightmare that passed itself off as a pub. Sometimes downwards is the only reasonable, respectful place to go.

Second, I couldn't express what we'd just seen meant to me. Oh, I could talk – I blathered every cliché and hyperbolic banality I could come up with – I just couldn't communicate what I actually felt. Because what I wanted to convey was my literal awe at being in Dylan's presence. Awe – something I'd experienced maybe twice before in my entire life and might never experience again. But because probably the week previous I'd said something along the lines of "Wow, what an awesome veggie burger" or "Awesome – I'll see you there at ten o'clock," I'd forfeited the right to use that particular, perfect adjective and was left instead with my impotent, because largely inarticulate, feelings.

When Joseph Conrad reminded his readers as much as himself that "it is only through complete, unswerving devotion to the perfect blending of form and substance; it is only through an unremitting, never-discouraged care for the shape and ring of sentences that an approach can be made to plasticity, to colour; and the light of magic suggestiveness may be brought to play for an evanescent instant over the commonplace surface of words: of the old, old words, worn thin, defaced by ages of careless usage," he wasn't arguing for the supremacy of some kind of hyper-exclusive art-for-art's sake aesthetic. Quite the opposite. What he was doing was pleading with us not to let lazy language rob of us our experiences, our emotions, our lives. "In the prison of his days," Auden wrote, "Teach the free man how to praise." For this to happen, the overriding lesson we need to learn – and relearn – is to free our minds.

DUTY

What is your duty? What each day requires.

    —Goethe

The word alone is disagreeable enough. *Fulfill your duty. It's your duty as a citizen. To each his own duty.* Then there are the innumerable, equally unpleasant variations, most of which are pounded into you when you're too young and stupid to fight back. *If a job is worth doing, it's worth doing right. Do unto others as you would have them do unto you. On my honour I promise that I will do my best, to do my duty to God and the Queen, to help other people at all times, and to carry out the spirit of the Scout Law.* What sensible person wouldn't want to run – or, rather, saunter – in the other direction, content to do and accomplish nothing?

With the exception of sports, I despised – literally, deeply, physically – almost everything my father cared about. And what he cared about most was doing dirty, repetitive, tedious jobs that nonetheless needed doing.

Washing the car. Cutting the lawn. Shoveling the driveway. Emptying the eavestroughs. Cleaning up the garage. He would have liked, naturally, his only son to assist him with these tasks, not only because it would have been respectful and right, but because the implicit lessons and values to be passed along – hard work, common sense, industriousness – would help to see his son through life, as they had him. I can't say that I possessed the foresight to intend it, but by the age of sixteen or so I'd somehow succeeded in making myself useless. It wasn't an instantaneous transformation – over time, I'd been incrementally demoted from apprentice lawn cutter to clippings bagger to cold drink retriever – but eventually my father resigned himself to his hopelessly impractical offspring. The upside was that he didn't have to share his chores and could guarantee that his hubcaps sparkled and that the trimmed and tidied front and back lawns would make the Tiger Stadium groundskeepers jealous.

It was fortunate that I wasn't yet aware of Baudelaire's *Intimate Journals*, or of his declaration that "To be a useful person has always appeared to me something particularly horrible," or else the already teenage-tested domestic peace of 90 Vanderpark Drive might have been further endangered. Bad enough for my parents my hopping pubescent hormones and my growing suspicion that avoiding doing boring, spirit-shrinking shit was what life was primarily about.

Besides, even when the task in question was actually worth doing – inarguably magnanimous acts, illustrious deeds, selfless sacrifices – it didn't take a Swift-sharpened satirist to detect that duty was more often spoken of than practiced. My father's repeated mantra that "Out of ten people – *any* ten people – one guy's a good guy, another guy's an asshole, and the rest are useless as tits on a nun" may not scan as well as Shakespeare's "Men's evil manners live in brass; their virtues/ We write in water," but his point was roughly the same and equally as true.

But you're not other people, you're never merely one out of ten. You're you. And if a healthy skepticism directed towards other people advising you what you should and should not be doing with your life is plainly necessary, so is satisfying one's sincerest scruples, however haphazardly-formed and indefinite. Even pimply-faced pseudo-nihilists know deep down that there are good things and that there are bad things and that the former are clearly preferable to the latter. As D.H. Lawrence's poem "Conscience" so succinctly encapsulates it:

Conscience
is sun-awareness
and our deep instinct
not to go against the sun.

And though we *can* stand a little more squarely in the light of the sun – arduously, incrementally, imperfectly – it's never the result of toting around weighty books of moral philosophy for quick consultation. People make us act better. Animals. Even rivers and trees and lakes. Sophocles wrote that "There is no witness so terrible – no accuser so powerful as the conscience which dwells within us." Listening to what our inner accuser has to say is usually the hardest and the first step.

For as long as I can remember I've liked to read my friends' journals and letters. When they went to the bathroom or when they went to get more beer from the refrigerator, I instantly – instinctively – became alert for an exposed notebook or a loose page. Maybe it was because I was an only child who never learned early on to respect the property and privacy of others, maybe it was because I was a writer-in-training without knowing it and couldn't resist such easy access to another human being's most intimate and interesting thoughts, but whatever the impetus, I couldn't resist reading what I knew I wasn't supposed to read. And I did know. There wasn't any measured justification I could trot out when my eye began to roam the room – I knew I wouldn't want anyone to do to me what I was doing to them, yet I did it again and again anyway.

By the time I met Brad Smith during second-year university, friends were few and alien journals and letters rare. Which was fine with me. I was twenty-one and freshly hometown-liberated; self-actualization, not socializing, was the objective *du jour*. Brad was enough of a freak to become a good friend – a fellow philosophy major with a predilection for cold beer and loud music – but his companionship was, I reasoned, complimentary rather than compulsory, childhood chumminess having now given way to unfussy adult acquaintanceship. But when a girlfriend's period was late, he was there to not so much talk it over as to wait around to see which colour the home pregnancy test turned. When I decided in the middle of third-year university to throw in the towel on academia and maybe try my hand at something a little less ... academic, he didn't counsel me one way or the other, but just patiently let me talk myself out and make the decision I needed to make before I could return to my studies and take both them and my life a little more seriously. And whenever the revelation of some new writer or musician or movie would compel me to explicate and proselytize (at length and volume I cringe to recall), he'd patiently listen until it was time for next week's next big discovery. "The language of friendship is not words but meanings," Thoreau wrote.

And when, once, while I was waiting for him to get out of the shower and get dressed so we could go out drinking, I spotted a notebook and flipped it open and immediately started reading. I was surprised to watch myself shut it just as impulsively as I had opened it. Brad's loyalty made me act loyally. His friendship made me a better friend.

And so one tries one's best not to go against the sun. To care about those who warrant it. To summon pity and generosity toward those who don't. To be as hard on oneself as one is on others. To perform one's chosen occupation as best as one can. To try to see the world that lies beyond one's nose. To reduce, reuse, recycle. All – and more – with great, great difficulty. Plutarch might have been right about how "Water continually dropping will wear hard rocks hollow," but most days it feels as if the rocks are winning. And all that dropping and dropping and dropping does tend to get a bit tiring.

One day my wife came home even more exhausted and exasperated than usual after spending too much time out in the world at large. She'd been carrying an empty coffee cup for over an hour searching in vain for a recycling bin, and emerged from the building in which she'd been into a parking lot so clogged with the leftover debris from a nearby Auto Show – discarded paper programs, crushed Styrofoam cups and plates, the clear plastic protective bags for some cheap giveaway trinket – that the blacktop was barely detectable. Three football fields of casually cast off crap, and her with a cramp in her right thumb from lugging around a single coffee cup. "You try to do the right thing, and then you see something like that and you wonder what's the point," she said before collapsing onto the couch. I didn't ask her what had happened to her cup.

Such crises of faith need not be as palpable at source as the physical destruction of the planet – the ostensibly ethereal can drive one to the couch (or worse) as well. Occasionally, for example, I'm foolish enough to stick my head outside my burrow to sniff the cultural winds, only to be rewarded with the customary stench of middlebrow mediocrity, which in my particular professional sphere manifests itself most conspicuously in the sort of highbrow Harlequin fiction that reliably reaches the top of the bestseller lists and gets nominated every year for the larger literary awards that the Canadian culture industry has cooked up to help perpetuate the necessary illusion that Canadian society genuinely cares about literature. The sort of fiction, in other words, that has inevitably led me at some point during the writing of every one of my novels to realize that what I have written will almost certainly be unofficially but no less effectively disqualified for prize consideration by that year's distinguished arbiters of taste, their tender sensibilities no doubt chafed by some damning reference of mine to either bodily functions (because we all know that people in works of literature don't go to the bathroom) or popular culture (because we all know that people in works of literature spend the majority of their time occupied not with jobs and families and television, but with either travelling to remote countries looking for lost lovers or children or else sitting in abandoned lighthouses alternately listening to the mournful sounds of the sea and brooding upon those eternal concerns of time, loss, and memory) or for simply failing to set said

novel in a sufficiently charmingly bucolic and/or fascina-
tingly exotic locale (because we all know that real literature
doesn't take place where most people actually live and
work and go to the mall and die).

Hence one can't nod emphatically enough along with
Emerson's assertion that "People do not deserve to have
good writing, they are so pleased with the bad." Hence one
crawls back into one's burrow. Again.

But not for long. As Martin Luther purportedly said,
"Even if I knew that tomorrow the world would end, I
would still plant my little apple tree." Planting new trees
and recycling your coffee cup and writing and reading
good literature are in and of themselves good things and
worthwhile actions, regardless of whether or not the world
as we know it will continue for very much longer or
whether the majority of people can be bothered to pay attention. "One ought to seek out virtue for its own sake,"
Diogenes argued, "without being influenced by fear or
hope, or by any external influence. Moreover, in that does
happiness consist."

And even if the good things we do aren't always done
as well as we would like or aren't ultimately as good as we'd
like to believe they are, this doesn't mean they're not worth
doing, that they're not worth the effort. So sometimes you
can't be bothered to scrape the hardened peanut butter out
of the bottom of the jar and consequently toss it into the garbage pail instead of the recycling bin – the bin is brimming
full of other items that you *did* recycle. So the eggs you eat at
the greasy spoon you like so much because the portions are
big and the prices are low aren't free range – the ones you
eat at home always are. So some of the films you gushed
over as an undergraduate for their iconoclastic quirkiness

and bold experimentalism you now recognize for the pretentious puffery they clearly are – at least you were willing to pay your money to sit and listen and watch and try to learn and grow.

Seneca was many admirable things: foremost, of course, a Roman Stoic philosopher, but also a statesman, a dramatist, a humorist, the tutor and later advisor to emperor Nero, and, as part of the Pisonian conspiracy to assassinate this last of the Julio-Claudian emperors, forced to commit a noble suicide. He was also, like most men of property of his time and place, a slave owner. As obviously regrettable – inexcusable – as this is, it wasn't unusual ("Some men are by nature free," Aristotle wrote, "and others slaves, and for these slavery is both expedient and right"). What was unusual were Seneca's unconventional views on slavery, which, though they may sound self-evident, many of his contemporaries judged plainly wrong and even offensively, dangerously radical.

> "He's a slave." But he may have the spirit of a free man. "He's a slave." But is that really to count against him? Show me a man who isn't a slave; one is a slave to sex, another to money, another to ambition; all are slaves to hope or fear. I could show you a man who has been a Consul who is a slave to his "little old woman," a millionaire who is the slave of a little girl in domestic service. I could show you some highly aristocratic young men who are utter slaves to stage artistes. And there's no state of slavery more disgraceful than one which is self-imposed. So you needn't allow yourself to be deterred by the snobbish people I've been talking about from showing a good humour to-

ward your slaves instead of adopting an attitude of ar-
rogant superiority towards them.

"We work in the dark," Henry James wrote " – we do
what we can – we give what we have." Seneca's participation in the institution of slavery unquestionably kept him in
partial darkness; his rare, heretical views on this same institution brought him – and everyone who came into contact
with them – a little further into the light. Every human being
lives in his or her own particular darkness. The struggle to
stand in the light, or a few millimeters closer to it, is equally
unique.

HOME

He is happiest, be he king or peasant, who finds peace in his home.

—Goethe

Everybody knows that travel stimulates the mind, expands one's perspective, encourages broadminded-ness and tolerance. Everybody knows that travel is a sure sign of worldliness, wisdom, sophistication. Everybody, as usual, is wrong.

Certainly travel has its benefits. It's good to discover, for instance, that although people may dress differently and eat different foods and drive on the other side of the road, they're all identifiably a part of the same essentially boorish, selfish, clueless species. It's also important to occasionally leave behind one's boring routines and staid sur-roundings and insipid friends in order to achieve some geographically-gained perspective, if for no other reason than to gladly return to one's boring routines and staid surroundings and insipid friends because travelling is always eventually even *more* boring, *more* staid, and *more* insipid.

But travel *qua* travel, construed as an edifying activity, is as shallow and fundamentally class-based as those who propound the $300, five-course dinner as some sort of cultural achievement. Socrates identified himself as one of those who ate to live as opposed to one who lived to eat. Similarly, Horace warned of those who "change their climate, not their disposition or soul, [when they] run beyond the sea." Dr. Johnson was even more indicting: "As the Spanish proverb says, 'He who would bring home the wealth of the Indies must carry the wealth of the Indies with him.' So it is in travelling: a man must carry knowledge with him, if he would bring home knowledge." Besides, as Socrates observed, "See one promontory, one mountain, one sea, one river, and see all." And that was 2,500 years before the first McDonald's opened up for business in downtown Prague.

Clichés are to be avoided in one's speech and writing, but should be paid careful attention to as rare indicators of candor in others. *A man's house is his castle. A house is not a home. Home is where the heart is. There's no place like home.* Trite, all of them, but true nonetheless. People may exaggerate and lie outright about the significance that art or spirituality plays in their lives, or how much they're concerned about the less fortunate members of their community, but there's no reason to doubt anyone who claims that at day's end they can't wait to get home. It may be partially because they can't stand to be at work anymore, of course, but it's also because, at its best, home is a temporary sanctuary, a hallowed place of recuperation and rejuvenation, a warm and familiar respite from an often cold and strange world. No one feels more comfortable than in their own bed, with all of their own stuff surrounding them. Your first adolescent sleepover teaches you that, no matter how good a friend someone is or how nice their house is, the way other people go about their business in their own space is sometimes just plain weird. Everyone else's house has a funny smell to it.

Sometimes a lifetime's richest memories are made in the humblest of homes. From the age of seven I grew up in the suburbs, and once I left at age nineteen I did everything I could to ensure that I never lived there again. Despite the oppressive uniformity of architecture and attitudes, however, I've never felt more snug or safe than when I was a child and the furnace would whoosh on in the middle of a bitingly-cold February night, buried somewhere deep underneath the small mountain of blankets my mother would tuck me in under, my parents right across the hall just in case there was anything in the world I needed. Although I'm the one paying the gas bill now and feel that I can sometimes actually see one hundred dollar bills floating on the currents of hot air coming out of the bedroom heat vent and just as swiftly being carried right out through the bedroom window, there's a residual throb of cozy comfort that calms and caresses me every time my own furnace comes on. Anthony Burgess opined that being faithful to the cuisine one was brought up on probably constitutes as satisfactory a definition of patriotism as any. It takes more than a passport and a packed suitcase to leave one's home behind.

Even those famous exiles compelled (whether from without or within) to flee home and country never leave entirely. The every-year louder and louder bells and whistles that mark June 16, 1904, Bloomsday, the day that James

Joyce chose to set his humdrum Irish odyssey, *Ulysses*, is a memorial, a party, an opportunity for university professors and other cultural bureaucrats to drink too much and not feel guilty. Like big-prize, high-publicity literary awards, it's good for the business end of art, but has absolutely nothing to do with its real reason for existing: Joyce's novel's ability to move, to unsettle, to – hopefully – even transform the lives of individual readers.

Joyce himself was an exceedingly private man. His life revolved around three rarely varying things: writing, home and family, and alcohol. Like his adored Daedulus, he was a master builder, manufacturing a comfortable home life for himself wherever his family ended up, a place where he could continue doing the things he loved to do surrounded by the people whom he loved and cared for. Visitors to the Joyce home were invariably surprised at how thoroughly lower middle-class it seemed (tacky pictures on the walls; mass-produced furniture; the smell of cooking in every room) – not so different, in fact, from Joyce's childhood home – and how Joyce, if the guest was either Irish or had recently been to Ireland, would grill him or her for Dublin gossip or want to engage them in a discussion of who was that country's finest singer of popular songs.

One can't help but recall Stephen's epiphany in *A Portrait of the Artist as a Young Man* when "The faint sour stink of rotted cabbages came towards him from the kitchen . . . He smiled to think that it was this disorder, the misrule and confusion of his father's house and the stagnation of vegetable life, which was to win the day in his soul." Genuine artists don't flee the familiar, everyday world, no matter how malodorous or carnal; rather, they embrace it, transforming it through their heightened craft into the very essence of their art. Even though by his mid-twenties Joyce was more or less a permanent exile, he never really left Dublin or the lower middle-class home he grew up in. Not incidentally, he wrote about little else.

Joyce's greatest work, *Ulysses*, is one of those books that everyone knows and has an opinion about but few have read. For a change, this isn't entirely the fault of the world. As Anthony Burgess observed, "No face shines through the novels of James Joyce, and this is disturbing" for most readers. This, because "[the majority of novel readers] agree in finding many novels too wordy; words, a necessary evil in the days of primitive art, are rendered supererogatory by the new, mostly visual, media . . . Most novel-readers want to get at the content of a novel without the intermediacy of a kind of writing that seems to obtrude, rivaling the plot in its claim to be looked at." To begin to understand – and, more importantly, enjoy – *Ulysses* is to realize that its main character is not Leopold or Molly Bloom or Stephen Daedalus, but the English language itself, both in terms of what it can and cannot be made to do.

That said, in spite of its ultra-literary nature (in both design and effect), *Ulysses* remains, at its core, a paean to domesticity, a long, complex poem in prose celebrating the comforting banality of everyday life, a book that begins at the breakfast table and ends in the bedroom. The first time the reader meets Leopold Bloom – the character who launched ten thousand scribbling Ph.D students – he's taking a moment from preparing his wife's morning meal to feed their cat. It's a scene of such shimmering domestic triviality – particularly in comparison to the various high-wire linguistic, symbolic, and thematic acts that surround it – it virtually sanctifies itself by virtue of its very ordinariness.

Kidneys were in his mind as he moved about the kitchen softly, righting her breakfast things on the humpy tray. Gelid light and air were in the kitchen but out of doors gentle summer morning everywhere. Made him feel a bit peckish.

The coals were reddening.

Another slice of bread and butter; three, four: right. She didn't like her plate full. Right. He turned from the tray, lifted the kettle off the hob and set it sideways on the fire. It sat there, dull and squat, its spout stuck out. Cup of tea soon. Good. Mouth dry.

The cat walked stiffly round a leg of the table with tail on high.

—Mkgnao!

—O, there you are, Mr. Bloom said, turning from the fire.

Joyce might have claimed that he wanted to keep puzzled university professors busy for hundreds of years, but making breakfast for the family and playing with the cat and keeping the coals hot are what his much-discussed, not-enough-read novel is really about.

The first address that was mine and mine alone was a fourth-floor university dorm room – four cement block walls painted traffic-light yellow in an attempt to soften the aesthetic blow (the attempt failed), with a cot, a chair, a closet, and a small beer fridge beside the head of the bed to keep my jar of peanut butter and cans of beer, and a washroom at the end of the hall that I shared with fifteen other concrete hive dwellers. But it was mine. I didn't make the bed if I didn't feel like it. I slept with the drapes open. I left the radio on CJRT, the jazz station, whenever I went to class (although I wasn't particularly fond of jazz, it seemed like a Toronto thing to do). I stayed up half the night reading books that weren't on any of my course syllabi while managing to keep myself going by eating cold pizza in bed at three a.m. and drinking Diet Pepsi right out of the 1.5 litre bottle.

Sometimes it was a little overwhelming to remember that just outside my window there were millions of other people going about *their* lives in *their* homes in the way *they* wanted – which, the newspapers daily confirmed, sometimes meant robbing and stabbing and shooting and murdering – but inside my tiny concrete bunker I felt safe, or at least safe enough, fulfilling with my first attempt at living alone what the poet William Cowper wished for: "O to have a lodge in some vast wilderness,/ Some boundless contiguity of shade,/ Where rumors of oppression and deceit,/ Of unsuccessful and successful wars,/ Might never reach me more." They might have reached me, but they stayed outside the door. My door.

A population of one can certainly make for a happy home, but a home is happier if the right combination of people and animals manage to mix together to make it a more alive and loving place. I'm fortunate to have been with the same partner for the last twenty years and to be on the second of two happy, healthy dogs. "One of the oldest human needs," Margaret Mead wrote, "is having someone to wonder where you are when you don't come home at night," and I know I'm lucky both to have somewhere to go home to and someone there to worry about me. But there are limits to how much one should be tamed, I always believed. I never, for instance, thought my bar-going days would ever end.

A good neighborhood bar has always provided a way to get out of the house while still feeling at home. A place where human contact can be renewed easily, but at the end of the night you still share the liberating anonymity of strangers. But there comes a time when, unless the drunk slobbering in your ear is the drunk you've known for ten years and whose wedding you've been to and whose kids you've bought birthday gifts for, it begins to seem not quite worth the walk to the end of the street. Add in too frequently loud, bad music and overpriced drinks, and you might finally be getting old.

Then we bought a couch. To most, it might not sound like a major investment, but we'd put it off for years. We rarely had enough people over to necessitate more than the two chairs in our library *cum* music-listening room, and although we always had enough money to keep a roof over our heads, there was seldom enough left over at month's end to fill up the rooms it kept (mostly) warm and dry. But when we did finally make the big purchase – second-hand and relatively cheap, but brown and comfy, as all couches should be – the second phase of my drinking life suddenly and unexpectedly materialized. Instead of the barroom, we now had the couch, and with my wife at one end and myself at the other and our dog – sleeping – in the middle, it turned out that all you needed to have a night out at home was a bottle or two of wine and a few choice record albums. For nearly a year afterward, whenever I'd occasionally stop at my local bar, someone would tell me they'd thought I'd quit drinking or that I'd been in jail. Nah, I'd say, I've just been hanging out at home.

In *Don Juan*, Byron remarks:

'Tis sweet to hear the watch-dog's honest bark
Bay deep-mouth'd welcome as we draw near home:
'Tis sweet to know there is an eye will mark
Our coming, and look brighter when we come.

It's the stuff of sappy films and maudlin power ballads, but that doesn't make it any less true. We all want the same things: acknowledgment; inclusion; appreciation. We all want to go home.

DEATH

There *is* that. Extinction, obliteration, annihilation. No matter how many reasons to live one has and no matter how happy one has been cultivating them, one is going to die. Just like the fish gasping and flopping on the bottom of the boat, just like the squirrel squashed in the middle of the street, just like everyone who came before you and everyone who will come along afterward. "Death is a debt which every man must pay," wrote Euripides. And some find this fee a little off-putting. Some find it a little more than that.

Life, Sartre claimed, has no meaning the moment "you have lost the illusion of being eternal." And even though this core existentialist attitude does carry with it the distinctly adolescent odour of "If you won't play my way, I'm taking my toys and going home," it's undeniable that, as Sartre's fellow advocate of the absurd Albert Camus maintained, "That nostalgia for unity, that appetite for the absolute illustrates the essential impulse of the human drama." Illustrating it even better is the following Stephen Crane poem:

> I saw a man pursuing the horizon;
> Round and round they sped.
> I was disturbed at this;
> I accosted the man.
> "It is futile," I said,
> "You can never—"
>
> "You lie," he cried,
> And ran on.

The good news is that because human beings are intrinsically meaning-needing and meaning-making machines, we get up to all sorts of fascinating and sometimes even very useful busyness – art, philosophy, religion, to name only a few. The bad news is that when we apply this same passion for purpose and meaning and accomplishment to our ultimate standing in the cosmos, we can't help but feel as if we're lacking significance and self-worth. Here's Crane again, once more hitting the existential nail squarely (and painfully) on its head:

> A man said to the universe:
> "Sir, I exist!"
> "However," replied the universe,

"The fact has not created in me
A sense of obligation."

Confronted with this universe of cold indifference,
human beings, according to Camus, have three options: suicide, a leap of faith, or recognition. As Wilfred Sheed so pith-
ily put it, "Suicide is . . . the sincerest form of criticism life
gets." It's not just a case of taking one's toys and going
home, but breaking all of the toys and burning down the
house while one is at it.

One can also take Kierkegaard's "leap of faith,"
wherein one embraces a non-rational meaning to life (e.g., a
religion that posits personal immortality). Camus, however,
considered the leap of faith simply another form of suicide –
in this case, "philosophical suicide" – and no more an
honest and satisfactory solution to the question of life's
meaning than the physical variety.

Finally, one can choose to recognize and embrace the
apparent meaninglessness of existence, with one's freedom
– and dignity and meaning – lying in one's willing acceptance of life's absurdity. "The only way to deal with an
unfree [i.e., indifferent] world," Camus concludes, "is to
become so absolutely free that your very existence is an act
of rebellion." For the rebel, then, "If there is sin against life, it
consists . . . in hoping for another life and in eluding the
implacable grandeur of this life." All of which boils down
to: you're going to die, nothing you did or believed in or
loved is going to survive, but at least you didn't kid yourself
otherwise. Honesty is the free man or woman's pride and
consolation.

The attempt to soothe the sting of death and life's resultant evanescence has been undertaken in various other,

far less systematic ways. To begin with, one argument goes, how appealing would death's elimination really be? Isn't it likely that life would eventually become one long sickening déjà vu, an exhaustingly endless rerun starring you and always all about you always doing and thinking and feeling the very same things? H.L. Mencken thought so: "When I die I shall be content to vanish into nothingness ... No show, however good, could conceivably be good forever." Charles Sanders Pierce believed there was another reason to be thankful for human mortality: mendacity. "If man were immortal," he argued, "he could be perfectly sure of seeing the day when everything in which he had trusted should betray his trust, and, in short, of coming eventually to hopeless misery. He would break down, at last, as every good fortune, as every dynasty, as every civilization does. In place of this we have death." Besides, what rare individual would be capable of not only being appreciative of immortality, but actually deserving of such an extraordinary gift? The once very popular, now virtually unknown British novelist Susan Ertz held that "Millions long for immortality who do not know what to do with themselves on a rainy Sunday afternoon." Faced with an eternity of rainy Sunday afternoons – particularly if compelled to spend them at Bed, Bath, and Beyond – extinction doesn't seem so bad after all.

There's also the argument for death's outright irrelevance ("Death is nothing to us," Epicurus argued. "For what has been dissolved has no sense-experience, and what has no sense-experience is nothing to us"). There's the contention that the trouble actually comes from viewing death myopically ("The day which we fear as our last is but the birthday of eternity," Seneca reasoned). There's the reminder that death is the great equalizer, the ultimate democratizer ("And they die an equal death," Homer pointed out, "the idler and the man of mighty deeds"). There's the potentially consoling logic that one's death means the elimination of life's pains and worries ("Death is a release from the impressions of sense," Marcus Aurelius contended, "and from impulses that make us their puppets, from the vagaries of the mind, and the hard service of the flesh." Emily Bronte put it more simply: "Oh, for the time when I shall sleep/ Without identity"). There's also glib wit and sundry other ironic forms of whistling past the awaiting graveyard ("Death is a very dull, dreary affair," Somerset Maugham opined, "and my advice to you is to have nothing whatever to do with it"). And so on.

None of which, of course, anyone believes. Not really. Not enough to make much of a difference, anyway. Even the most carefully constructed, seemingly impervious philosophical system can crumble to dusty dogma in the middle of the night. "Against other threats it is possible to provide security," Epicurus observed, "but on account of death all of us humans inhabit a city without walls." More than our opposable thumbs and our talent for serenely deluding ourselves, what most clearly separates us from all the other animals is awareness of our own mortality. Death, Montaigne wrote, "frightens us, it is a continual source of torment which cannot be alleviated at all. There is no place from which it may not come to us; we may turn our heads constantly this way and that as in a suspicious country: death always hangs over us."

Not being able to forget death or to argue away its solemn significance, then, why not simply accept it and actually attempt to utilize it in a way that might increase one's happiness while one is still alive? When life hands you the prospect of a stopped heart and rotting flesh and an eternity of oblivion, why not make lemonade? Or something else equally revitalizing.

When you're twelve years old, summer holidays seem almost as good as Christmas. True, there aren't any gifts, but there's freedom – two entire months of it. Too old to be supervised by your mother or a babysitter anymore (quite the opposite, in fact – if you *do* linger around the house, instead of maternal gratitude, what you're more likely to hear is, "Why don't you go outside and play?"), you're also too young to have to get a job and so begin to learn the hard lesson that time to do what you want is the greatest valuable one can possess, and that money is most useful when it helps to purchase more of it. School is even almost fun when summer vacation nears, softball games occasionally substituted for math class and the windows wide open in the classroom to admit the summer smell of freshly cut grass, and a full day off for field day, your mum giving you a whole dollar to buy hot dogs and orange pop and potato chips.

And at first it *is* good. Better than good: amazing. Staying up late to watch all of the shows everyone has been talking about, sleeping in until whenever you feel like waking up, rounding up your best friends every morning to play road hockey or baseball or to bicycle over to the recreation centre to go swimming. You never miss the dingling Dickie Dee who pedals his way through the subdivision every sweltering afternoon – some sweat-soaked teenager working for $2.15 an hour – and every day is Saturday and it seems almost unbelievable that September and school will ever come around again.

Inevitably, though, who wins the game matters less and less each day; the TV shows are all stupid or reruns or both; your best friends turn out not be best friends after all but jerks; and, worst of all, you're bored. You're not in school, but somehow you're bored anyway. Every morning you drag yourself to the kitchen table to eat your Sugar Crisp and wonder what the hell you're going to do all day, how you're going to fill up all of those empty hours. By the time August crawls around, your mother has to chase you from the couch where you're content, if not exactly happy, to lie and watch *F-Troop* and *Petticoat Junction* and *The Price is Right* all afternoon, shows you've never even liked. It's almost enough to make you want school to start up again.

But snow days. Unforeseen, always astonishing snow days. When you wake up to the report on the radio (*The following schools are closed . . .*) and can't wait to go outside and get a game going or grab your Crazy Carpet or anything, really, just as long as you hurry up and start doing it *right now* because there's no way in h-e-double-hockey-sticks they'll cancel school two days in a row and time is ticking, ticking on today. No one is ever bored on a snow day. Stolen days are always the best.

If even our holidays as children are made richer and more meaning-filled – made more alive – when we know they're limited, why shouldn't the same apply to our very lives? Instead of death being a reason to negate life – a sour shadow that casts everything it touches in acid gloom – why not view it instead as a spur to help ensure that we try to do more, work harder, go slower, love more freely, live less reservedly? "The certain prospect of death could sweeten every life with a precious and fragrant drop of levity,"

Nietzsche believed. " – and now you strange apothecary souls have turned it into an ill-tasting drop of poison that makes the whole of life repulsive." Death isn't life's repudiation. On the contrary – without it, life would lose much of its meaning.

Unfortunately, the nearest most of us come to truly recognizing and relishing our lives is when they're directly threatened – by a life-threatening disease, for example, or a near fatal accident. It is then that the words of Ecclesiastes aren't merely pretty pious prose, but are a very real challenge and a heartfelt call to action:

> Enjoy life with the woman whom you love all the days of your fleeting life which He has given to you under the sun; for this is your reward in life and in your toil in which you have labored under the sun. Whatever your hand finds to do, do *it* with *all* your might; for there is no activity or planning or knowledge or wisdom in Sheol where you are going.

The most expensive record albums I own aren't necessarily my favourites. They are expensive because they're rare. I have other records I listen to more often and value higher aesthetically, but the ones that were the hardest to locate and the most difficult to acquire are the ones I esteem the most. Alan Wilson and Bob Hite, the two main creative forces behind the blues-rock band Canned Heat, were obsessive blues record collectors long before they were full-time musicians. The story goes that they were so fanatical, when either of them found another copy of one of their most cherished discs, they would buy it just so they could break it in two and make their own copy that much rarer. They've both been dead for a long time now, so no one knows for sure if the story is apocryphal. I like to believe it's true.

NOTES

Introduction

P.17 *Life, friends, is boring:* John Berryman, *The Dream Songs*, Farrar, Strauss and Giroux, 1969, p 16

P.17 *Absence of occupation is:* William Cowper, *The Life and Letters of William Cowper*, Longman, Rees, and Co., 1835, p 571

P.19 *The thought of suicide: The Viking Book of Aphorisms, A Personal Selection by W.H. Auden and Louis Kronenberger*, Dorset Press, 1981, p 19

P.21 *Disease makes health pleasant:* Heraclitus, *Heraclitus: The Cosmic Fragments*, with Introduction, Text, and Translation by G.S. Kirk, Cambridge University Press, 1975, p 130

P.21-22 *I should not talk:* Henry David Thoreau, *Walden*, J.M Dent & Sons, 1943, p 1

P.22 *Shall I tell you:* Seneca, *Letters from a Stoic*, Selected and Translated with an Introduction by Robin Campbell, Penguin Books, 1969, p 98

P.22-23 *Philosophy takes as her: Ibid,* p 171

P.23 *There is but one:* Albert Camus, *The Myth of Sisyphus*, Translated by Justin O'Brien, Vintage Books, 1955, p 3

P.23 *Death is not the:* *The Oxford Dictionary of Medical Quotations*, Edited by Peter McDonald, Oxford University Press, 2005, p 94

Work

P.27 *Why should I let:* Philip Larkin, *Collected Poems*, Edited with an Introduction by Anthony Thwaite, The Marvell Press and Faber and Faber, 1990, p 89

P.28 *Man finds nothing so:* Blaise Pascal, *Pensées*, Translated with an Introduction by A.J. Krailsheimer, Penguin Books, 1995, p 208

P.29 *Work is often the:* James Parton, *Life of Voltaire*, Houghton Mifflin, 1881, p 332

P.30 *Derive happiness in oneself:* Jack Flam, *Matisse on Art*, University of California Press, 1995, p 174

P.31 *die like a dog:* Gustave Flaubert, *The Letters of Gustave Flaubert 1830-1857*, Selected, Edited, and Translated by Francis Steegmuller, 1980, p 161

P.31 *Work, work, write – write: Ibid*, p 35

P.31 *Do not brood. Immerse: Ibid*, p 143

P.31 *I continue my slow: Ibid*, p 36

P.32-33 *I'll tell you which: Ibid*, p 159

P.34 *[w]e weren't drafted, we:* Mordecai Richler, *Broadsides*, Viking Press, 1990, p 8

P.34 *[my] father, a failed: Ibid*

P.34 *Blessed is who has:* Thomas Carlyle, *Past and Present*, Chapman and Hall, 1872, p 262

P.35 *Pleasure in the job: Dictionary of Quotations*, Edited by Manoranjan Kumar, S.B. Nangia, 2008, p 253

P.35 *A man cannot make: The Columbia Dictionary of Quotations*, Edited by Robert Andrews, Columbia University Press, 1993, p 192

Love

P.39 *They fuck you up:* Larkin, *Collected Poems*, p 180

P.41 *The soul selects her:* Emily Dickinson, *The Complete Poems of Emily Dickinson*, Edited by Thomas H. Johnson, Little Brown, 1960, p 143

P.41 *It takes patience to:* George Santayana, *The Life of Reason or The Phases of Human Progress*, Charles Scribner's Sons, 1919, p 45

P.42 *At times I wonder: Ten Thousand Leaves*, Translated from the Japanese by Harold Wright, The Overlook Press, 1986, p 46

P.42 *The storms one so:* Flaubert, *The Letters of Flaubert 1830-1857*, p 143.

P.42 *you should divide your: Ibid*, p 197

P.42 *The sexual embrace can: The Routledge Dictionary of Religious and Spiritual Quotations*, Edited by Geoffrey Parrinder, Routledge, 2000, p 163

P.42 *Love comforeth like sunshine*, William Shakespeare, *The Riverside Shakespeare*, Textual Editor G. Blakemore Evans, Houghton Mifflin, 1974, p 1714

P.43 *i am through you:* e.e. cummings, *22 and 50 Poems*, Norton, 2001, p 94

P.43 *Belief in the existence:* Simone Weil, *Gravity and Grace*, Translated by Arthur Wills, Bison Books, 1997, p 113

P.44 *Since we are alone: Ten Thousand Leaves,* p 35

P.46 *If from your mouth: Ibid,* p 84

Intoxication

P.47 *Man, being reasonable, must:* Byron, *Byron: Selected Poetry and Prose*, Edited by Donald A. Low, Routledge, 1995, p 247

P.47 *Drunkenness is nothing but:* Seneca, *Letters From a Stoic,* p 143

P.47 *Drunkenness is temporary suicide:* Bertrand Russell, *The Conquest of Happiness*, Unwin Paperbacks, 1984, p 19

P.48 *One of the disadvantages: Dictionary of Quotations,* Edited by Connie Robertson, Wordsworth Editions, 1998, p 188

P.48 *I had not taken:* William Burroughs, *Naked Lunch: the Restored Text*, Edited by James Grauerholz and Barry Miles, Grove, 2001, p 202

P.48 *Dope never helped anybody:* John White, *Billie Holiday: Her Life and Times*, Spellmount 1987, p126

P.48 *Wine gives a man:* James Boswell, *The Life of Samuel Johnson*, H. Washbourne, 1857, p 392

P.48 *Champagne, if you are:* V.V.B. Rama Rao, *Graham Greene's Comic Vision*, Reliance Publishing House, 1990, p 172

P.49 *Tobacco and alcohol, delicious: The Columbia Book of Quotations,* p 849

P.49 *Wreath the bowl/With:* Thomas Moore, *The Poetical Works of Thomas Moore*, Edited by A.D. Godley, Humphrey Milford-Oxford University Press, 1924, p 213

P.50 *I drink only to: Quote Unquote*, Lotus Press, Edited by M.P Singh, 2006, p 123

P.50 *Malt does more than:* A.E. Houseman, *The Collected Poems of A.E. Houseman*, Jonathan Cape, 1948, p 88

P.52 *That I am mortal: Poems from the Greek Anthology*, translated by Dudley Fitts, New Directions, 1956, p 130

P.53 *For me, drugs are:* Robert Greenfield, *Dark Star: An Oral Biography of Jerry Garcia,* Broadway Books, 1996, p 169

P.54 *He called* [heroin] *his: Ibid*, p 205

P.54-55 *We've been running on:* Blair Jackson, *Jerry Garcia: An American Life*, Penguin Books, 2000, p 407

P.55 *I have taken more:* Chris Wrigley, *Winston Churchill: A Biographical Companion*, ABC-CLIO, Inc., 2002, p 13

P.55-56 *A good sherris sack:* Shakespeare, *The Riverside Shakespeare*, p 912

P.56 *Aye, sir; to be: Ibid*, p 1154

P.56 *No man is a:* Boswell, *The Life of Samuel Johnson*, p 529

P.56 *The true function of:* Cyril Connolly, *The Unquiet Grave*, Harper Colophon Books, 1973, p 1

P.56 *Oh, the joy of:* Cyril Connolly, *The Condemned Playground*, Macmillan Company, 1946, p 205

Art

P.59 *Culture is an instrument:* Deal W. Hudson and Matthew J. Mancicni, *Understanding Maritain*, Mercer University Press, 1987, p 171

P.60 *In all great art:* Brian McGuinness, *Approaches to*

Wittgenstein, Routledge, 2002, p 22

P.60 *The best is the enemy: Uncommon Sense*, Edited by Jospeh Telushkin, Shapolsky Publishers, 1987, p 203

P.60 *If you want a: 20th-Century Poetry & Poetics*, Edited by Gary Geddes, Oxford University Press, 1969, p 554

P.60 *the wise reader reads:* Vladimir Nabokov, *Lectures on Literature*, Edited by Fredson Bowers, Harcourt Brace Jovanovich, 1982, p 6

P.62 *the human incarnation of:* Craig Wright, *Listening to Western Music*, 2007, Schirmer, p 177

P.65 *Style is the ultimate: The Creative Process*, Edited and with an Introduction by Brewster Ghiselin, University of California Press, 1985, p 181

P.65 *The style is the:* Cleanth Brooks, *Fundamentals of Good Writing*, Fitts Press, 2007, p 459

P.65-66 *I got the idea: The Paris Review Interviews, 4th Series*, Edited by George Plimpton and Introduced by Wilfred Sheed, Penguin Books, 1976, 364-365

P.68 *The power of the:* Marianne Moore, *The Complete Poems of Marianne Moore*, Penguin, 1987, p 100

The Material World

P.70 *For the body at:* Edna St. Vincent Millay, *Collected Lyrics of Edna St. Vincent Millay*, Washington Square Press, 1966, p 144

P.71 *Imagination disposes of everything:* Pascal, *Pensées*, p 11

P.71 *The brain is wider than:* Dickinson, *The Complete Poems of Emily Dickinson*, p 312

P.72 *We think in generalities: Civilization's Quotations: Life's Ideal,*

Edited by Richard Alan Krieger, Algora, 2002, p 281

P.72 *If anything is sacred:* Whitman, *Leaves of Grass,* Signet Classic, 2000, p 86

P.72 *And nothing, not God: Ibid,* p 75

P.72 *I celebrate myself: Ibid,* p 22

P.72 *is commonest and cheapest:* Milton Hindus, *Walt Whitman: The Critical Heritage,* Routledge, 1997, p 39

P.72-73 *I believe a leaf: Walt Whitman & the World,* Edited by Gay Wilson Allen and Ed Folsom, University of Iowa Press, 1995, p 191

P.73 *Won't they try to:* Montaigne, *The Complete Essays of Montaigne,* Translated by Donald Frame, Stanford University Press, 1968, p 850

P.73 *They want to get: Ibid,* p 856

P.73 *When I dance, I: Ibid,* p 850

P.74 *The greatest wealth: Quote Unquote,* p 161

P.74 *the feeling of health:* Whitman, *Leaves of Grass,* p 24

P.74 *People who are always: Quote Unquote,* p 160

P.74 *To preserve health is: Civilization's Quotations: Life's Ideal,* p 308

P.74 *Sexuality is the lyricism:* Charles Baudelaire, *Intimate Journals,* Translated by Christopher Isherwood, City Lights Books, 1983, p 87

P.75 *Is it not an:* Montaigne, *The Complete Essays of Montaigne,* p 855

P.75 *What must first be:* J. Harvey Lomax, *The Paradox of Philosophical Education,* Lexington Books, 2003, p 16

P.75 *No one was ever:* Connolly, *The Unquiet Grave*, p 59

P.75 *Take rest; a field:* Ovid, *The Routledge Dictionary of Latin Quotations*, Routledge, 2005, p 19

P.75 *thou ape of death:* Shakespeare, *The Riverside Shakespeare*, p 1531

P.76 *velvet in his vertebrae:* Alfred Perles, *My Friend Henry Miller*, N. Spearmen, 1956, p 71

P.78 *All are but parts:* The Norton Anthology of English Literature, W.W. Norton & Company, 1975, p 1176

P.78 *Men argue, nature acts:* The Viking Book of Aphorisms, p 99

P.79 *I, who boast of:* Montaigne, *The Complete Essays of Montaigne*, p 849

Individuality

P.82 *Individualism is rather like:* Dictionary of Quotations, p 215

P.83 *[T]hey sit cool in:* Friedrich Nietzsche, *The Portable Nietzsche*, Edited and Translated by Walter Kaufmann, Penguin Books, 1985, p 237

P.83 *Individuality is freedom lived:* John Dos Passos, *Occasions and Protests*, H. Regnery Co, 1964, p 52

P.83-84 *Great poets seldom make:* Ezra Pound, *The Spirit of Romance*, New Directions, 2005, p 162

P.84 *We perceive and are:* Henry David Thoreau, *Early Spring in Massachusetts*, Houghton Mifflin, 1893, p 179

P.84 *Generally speaking, men are:* Periodical Literature in Eighteenth-Century America, Edited by Mark Kamrath and Sharon M. Davis, University of Tennessee Press, 2005, p 119

P.85-86 *Most prose writers [and]:* Allen Ginsberg, *Allen Verbatim*, Edited by Gordon Ball, McGraw-Hill Paperbacks, 1975, p. 151-153

P.86 *If I'm going to: America I AM Legends: Rare Moments and Inspiring Words*, Hay House, 2009, p 25

P.86 *To be nobody but: 20th-Century Poetry & Poetics*, p 438

P.86 *I would rather sit:* Thoreau, *Walden*, p 31

P.87 *It has been said:* Friedrich Nietzsche, *The Birth of Tragedy & The Genealogy of Morals*, Translated by Francis Golffing, Anchor Books, 1956, p 216

P.89 *That's where I'm going: Back to the Beach*, Edited by Kingsley Abbott, Helter Skelter Publishing, 2003, p 59

P.89 *I think it was:* Steven Gaines, *Heroes and Villains*, Da Capo Press, 1995, p 177

P.89 *Don't fuck with the: Ibid*, p 174

P.89 *acid alliteration:* Peter Ames Carlin, *Catch a Wave: The Rise, Fall & Redemption of the Beach Boys' Brian Wilson*, Rodale, 2006, p 114

P.90 *Ambition should be made:* Shakespeare, *The Riverside Shakespeare*, p 1121

Humour

P.92 *Common sense and a: Quote Unquote*, p 114

P.93 *Nothing is more curious:* Walter Leuba, *George Saintsbury*, Twayne Publishers, 1967, p 74

P.93 *A mysterious carriage of:* Laurence Sterne, *The Works of Laurence Sterne, in Five Volumes, Volume First*, John Myeth, 1854, p 33

P.93-94 *Imagination was given to: Quote Unquote*, p 164

P.94 *Twenty-one is the:* Anthony Burgess, *One Man's Chorus*, Selected with an introduction by Ben Forkner, Caroll and Graff Publishers, 1998, p 226

P.94-95 *when Kubrick made his: Ibid,* p 227

P.95 *The human race has: Worth Repeating: More than 5,000 Classic and Contemporary Quotes,* Edited by Bob Kelly, Kregel Academic, 2003, p 201

P.95 *Humor is perhaps a:* Lawrence C. Ross Jr., *The Ways of Black Folks: A Year in the Life of a People,* Kensington Publishing Corporation, 2004, p 273

P.97 *Analyzing humor is like:* Sol Steinmetz, *Semantic Antics: How and Why Words Change Meaning,* Random House, 2008, p 103

P.99 *Nothing shows a man's: Orient Book of Quotations,* Orient Paperbacks, 2008, p 112

P.99 *The earth laughs in:* Donald Yannella, *Ralph Waldo Emerson,* Twayne Publishers, 1982, p 77

Meaning

P.101 *as tedious as a:* Shakespeare, *The Riverside Shakespeare*, p 1543

P.102 *If we have our:* Nietzsche, *The Portable Nietzsche*, p 468

P.103 *This is the character:* Voltaire, *The Portable Voltaire*, Penguin Books, 1977, p 198

P.103 *an act of total:* Paul Tillich, *The Essential Tillich*, Edited by F. Forrester Church, University of Chicago Press, 1999, p 15

P.103 *Colour possesses me. I: The Diary of Paul Klee: 1898-1918,* Edited, with an Introduction by Felix Klee, University of California Press, p 297

P.104 *Be always drunken. Nothing:* Charles Baudelaire, *Paris Spleen,* Translated from the French by Louise Varase, New Directions, 1970, p 74

P.106 *One of the symptoms: Dictionary of Quotations,* p 253

P.106 *Patriotism is the last:* Bertrand Harris Bronson, *Johnson Agonistes and Other Essays,* University of California Press, 1946, p 24

P.107 *the child of ignorance:* William Hazlitt, *Sketches and Essays,* John Templeman, 1839, p 83

P.107 *A hurtful act is:* Weil, *Gravity and Grace,* p 123

P.107 *striving to find a:* Victor E. Frankl, *Man's Search for Meaning,* Pocket Books, 1973, p 154

P.107-108 *no instinct tells him:* Ibid, p 168

P.108 *People car[ing] more about: The Viking Book of Aphorisms,* p 61

Friendship

P.114 *Animals are such agreeable:* George Eliot, *Wit and Wisdom of George Eliot: with a Biographical Memoir,* Roberts Brothers, 1886, p 11

P.117 *A man's growth is:* Ralph Waldo Emerson, *Essays and Poems by Ralph Waldo Emerson,* Edited by Peter Norberg, Barnes and Noble Classics, 2004, p 205

P.118 *It is one of:* Ralph Waldo Emerson, *Emerson in his Journals,* Selected and edited by Joel Porte, Belknap, 1982, p 195

P.118 *One loyal friend is:* Daniel J. Hruschka, *Friendship: Development, Ecology, and Evolution of a Relationship,* University of California Press, 2010, p 102

P.118 *The only thing to:* Richard Warrington Baldwin Lewis, *Edith Wharton: A Biography*, Harper & Row, 1975, p 382

P.119 *It is not so:* Cyril Bailey, *The Greek Atomists and Epicurus*, Russell & Russell, 1964, p 519

P.119 *Most friendship is feigning:* Shakespeare, *The Riverside Shakespeare*, p 382

P.119 *one soul in two:* A.W. Price, *Love and Friendship in Plato and Aristotle*, Clarendon Paperbacks, 1990, p 111

P.120 *No one talks about:* Peter Kreeft, *Christianity for Modern Pagans*, Igantius Press, 1993, p 151

Solitude

P.121 *There are days when:* Quote Unquote, p 249

P.121 *I hold this to:* Dictionary of Quotations, p 352

P.122 *I think that I:* Henry David Thoreau, *I to Myself: An Annotated Selection from the Journal of Henry D. Thoreau*, Edited by Jeffrey S. Cramer, Yale University, 2007, p 313

P.122-123 *Society is commonly too:* Thoreau, *Walden*, p 120

P.123 *It seemed as if:* Ralph Waldo Emerson, *Selected Writings of Ralph Waldo Emerson*, Signet Classic, 2003, p 457

P.123-124 *I find it wholesome:* Thoreau, *Walden*, p 119

P.124 *You crowd around your:* Nietzsche, *The Portable Nietzsche*, p 172

P.125 *One must learn to:* Ibid, p 305

P.125 *Man loves company even:* Georg Christoph Lichtenberg, *Aphorisms*, Penguin Books, Translated with an Introduction and Notes by R.J. Hollingdale, 1990, p 171

P.126 *Solitude is not something:* Thomas Merton, *The Sign of Jonas*, Houghton Mifflin Harcourt, 2002, p 262

P.126 *The greatest events – they:* Nietzsche, *The Portable Nietzsche*, p 243

P.127 *bloodstains on his desk:* Blake Bailey, *A Tragic Honesty: The Life and Work of Richard Yates*, Picador, 2003, p 195

P.127-128 *It was, I believed: Ibid*, p 470

P.128 *the intellect of man:* W.B. Yeats, *The Collected Poems of W.B. Yeats*, Wordsworth Editions, 2000, p 209

P.128 *Nowhere can man find:* Marcus Aurelius, *Mediations*, Penguin Books, 1964, p 63

P.129 *The happiest of all: Quote Unquote*, p 250

The Critical Mind

P.132 *I am a poet:* Edmund Wilson, *Upstate*, Syracuse University Press, 1990, p 4

P.133 *learning, logic, and dramatic:* Edmund Wilson, *The Portable Edmund Wilson*, Edited, with an Introduction and notes by Lewis M. Dabney, The Viking Press, 1983, p 26

P.134 *Reading maketh a full:* Francis Bacon, *Francis Bacon: The Essays*, Oxford University Press, 1999, p 114

P.134 *I rejoice to concur:* Jeffrey Meyers, *Samuel Johnson: The Struggle*, Basic Books, 2008, p 451

P.134-135 *[W]hat I look for:* Alfred Kazin, *Contemporaries: The New and Revised Edition*, Horizon Press, 1982, p 7

P.135 *was hopelessly caught up:* Alfred Kazin, *New York Jew*, Syracuse University Press, 1996, p 26

P.136 *the worst thing one:* George Orwell, *George Orwell: Essays, Journals, and Letters, Volume Four,* Edited by Sonia Orwell and Ian Angus, A Nonpareil Book, 2000, p 138

P.137 *All that is necessary: Edmund Burke: Appraisals and Applications,* Edited by Daniel E. Ritchie, Transaction Publishers, 1990, p xiii

P.138 *One has to accept:* Seneca, *Letters from a Stoic,* p 197

Praise

P.139 *Against stupidity the Gods:* Claudia Pilling, Diana Schilling, Mirjam Springer, *Schiller,* Haus Publisher, 2005, p 97

P.139 *is safer than praise:* Emerson, *Essays and Poems by Ralph Waldo Emerson,* p 149

P.140 *[i]rony scratches her tired:* Jim Harrison, *The Beast That Time Forgot to Invent,* Atlantic Monthly Press, 2000, p 166

P.140 *Esteeming itself is of:* Nietzsche, *The Portable Nietzsche,* p 171

P.141 *I'd rather learn from:* e.e. cummings, *100 Selected Poems,* Grove Press, 1959, p 66

P.141 *You higher men, the:* Nietzsche, *The Portable Nietzsche,* p 407-408

P.142 *reconcil[ing] a high degree:* Harvey Cox, *The Feast of Fools,* Harper Colophon Books, 1970, p 28

P.143 *a poet's patience and: Nabokov at Cornell,* Edited by Gavriel Shapiro, Cornell University, 2003, p 122

P.143 *not about [gleaning] information:* Al Alvarez, *The Writer's Voice,* W.W. Norton & Company, 2005, p 17

P.143 *unlike any other voice: Ibid*

P.143-144 *finding your own voice: Ibid*, p 40

P.144 *listen . . . as attentively as: Ibid*, p 48

P.145 *defeats the curse which: The Norton Anthology of English Literature*, p 1818

P.145 *Take a commonplace, clean:* Ben Belitt, *The Forged Feature: Toward a Poetics of Uncertainty: New and Selected Essays*, Fordham University Press, p 218

P.148 *it is only through:* Joseph Conrad, *The Nigger of Narcissus and The End of the Tether*, Dell Publishing, 1960, p 27

P.148 *In the prison of:* W.H. Auden, *Collected Poems*, Edited by Edward Mendelson, Vintage International, 1991, p 249

Duty

P.151 *Men's evil manners live:* Shakespeare, *The Riverside Shakespeare*, p 1008

P.151 *There is no witness so: Civilization's Quotations*, p 20

P.153 *The language of friendship:* Jane Bennett, *Thoreau's Nature: Ethics, Politics and the Wild*, Sage Publications, 1994, p 24

P.153 *Water continually dropping will:* Plutarch, *Plutarch's Morals*, Translated from the Greek by Several Hands, Corrected and Revised by William Godwin, Little, Brown and Company, 1874, p 6

P.155 *People do not deserve:* Emerson, *Selected Writings of Ralph Waldo Emerson*, p 87

P.155 *One ought to seek:* C.D. Yonge and Keith Seddon, *A Summary of Stoic Philosophy*, Lulu, 2007, p 5

P.156 *Some men are by:* Aristotle, *Politics*, Translated by Benjamin Jowett, Cosimo Inc., 2008, p 368

P.156-157 *"He's a slave." But:* Seneca, *Letters From a Stoic*, p 95

P.157 *We work in the:* Henry James, *The Portable Henry James*, Penguin Books, Edited by John Auchard, 2004, p 126

Home

P.160 *change their climate, not: Civilization's Quotations*, p 7

P.160 *As the Spanish proverb:* Thomas M. Curley, *Sir Robert Chambers: Law, Literature, and Empire in the Age of Johnson*, University of Wisconsin Press, 1998, p 369

P.160 *See one promontory, one:* Robert Burton, *The Essential Anatomy of Melancholy*, General Publishing, 2002, p 91

P.163 *No face shines through:* Anthony Burgess, *Re Joyce*, Norton, 2000, p 25

P.165 *Oh to have a:* William Cowper, *The Poetical Works of William Cowper*, Edited by Henry Francis Cary, H.G. Bohn, 1864, p 62

P.165 *One of the oldest:* James L. Christian, *Philosophy: An Introduction to the Art of Wondering*, Wadsworth Publishing, 2005, p 148

Death

P.169 *Death is a debt:* Euripides, *Orestes and Other Plays*, Translated by Phillip Vellacott, Penguin Books, 1972, p 186

P.169 *you have lost the:* Jean-Paul Sartre, *The Wall and Other Stories*, Translated by Lloyd Alexander, New Directions, 1975, p 12

P.170 *That nostalgia for unity:* Abraham Sagi, *Albert Camus and the Philosophy of the Absurd*, Editions Rodopi, 2002, p 61

P.170 *I saw a man:* Stephen Crane, *Selected Prose and Poetry*, Introduction by William M. Gibson, Rinehart & Co, 1950, p 217

P.170-171 *A man said to: Ibid,* p 223

P.171 *Suicide is . . . the sincerest:* Wilfred Sheed, *The Good Word*, E.P. Dutton, 1978, p 68

P.171 *philosophical suicide:* Moya Langstaffe, *The Fiction of Albert Camus: A Complex Simplicity,* Peter Lang AG, 2007, p 24

P.171 *The only way to:* Zygmunt Bauman, *44 Letters from the Liquid Modern World,* Polity Press, 2010, p 184

P.172 *When I die I:* H.L. Mencken, *The Gist of Mencken: Quotations from America's Critic,* Edited by Mayo DuBasky, Scarecrow Press, 1990, p 203

P.172 *If man were immortal:* Charles Sanders Pierce, *The Essential Pierce 1867-1893,* Edited by Nathan Houser and Christian J.W. Kloesel, Indiana University Press, 1992, p 149

P.172 *Millions long for immortality: Philosophy: An Introduction to the Art of Wondering,* p 602

P.172 *Death is nothing to:* Philip de May, *Lucretius: Poet and Epicurean,* Cambridge University Press, 2009, p 72

P.172 *The day which we:* Charles Henry Stanley Davis, *Greek and Roman Stoicism and Some of its Disciples Epictetus, Seneca and Marcus Aurelius,* H.B. Turner and co., 1903, p 232

P.173 *And they die an:* Homer, *Iliad,* Translated by William Cullen Byrant, Fields, Osgoode, & Co., 1870, p 281

P.173 *Death is a release:* de May, *Lucretius: Poet and Epicurean,* p 72

P.173 *Oh, for the time:* Emily Bronte, *The Poems of Emily Bronte,* Edited by Barbara Llloyd-Evans, Barnes & Noble Books, 1992, p 57

P.173 *Death is a very:* Robert B. Taylor, *White Coat Tales: Medicine's Heroes, Heritage, and Misadventures*, Springer Science & Business Media, 2008, p 147

P.173 *Against other threats it:* Diskin Clay, *Lucretius and Epicurus*, Cornell University Press, 1983, p 186

P.173 *frightens us, it is:* Montaigne, *The Complete Essays of Montaigne*, p 57

P.175-176 *The certain prospect of:* Friedrich Nietzsche, *Basic Writings of Nietzsche*, Introduction by Peter Gay and Translated by Walter Kaufman, Modern Library Edition, 2000, p 165

SANDY NICHOLSON

Ray Robertson is the author of the novels *Home Movies, Heroes, Moody Food, Gently Down the Stream, What Happened Later,* and *David*, as well as a collection of non-fiction, *Mental Hygiene: Essays on Writers and Writing*. He is a contributing book reviewer to the *Globe and Mail*.